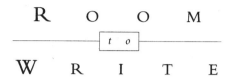

R O O M

t o

W R I T E

A Jeremy P. Tarcher/Putnam Book

published by

G. P. Putnam's Sons

New York

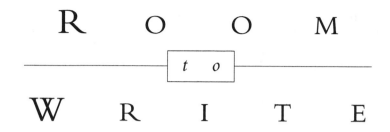

R O O M

t o

W R I T E

Daily Invitations to a Writer's Life

B O N N I   G O L D B E R G

Most Tarcher/Putnam books are available at special quantity discounts for bulk purchases for sales promotions, premiums, fund-raising, and educational needs. Special books or book excerpts also can be created to fit specific needs.

For details, write or telephone Special Markets, The Putnam Publishing Group, 200 Madison Avenue, New York, NY 10016; (212) 951-8891.

A JEREMY P. TARCHER/PUTNAM BOOK
Published by G. P. Putnam's Sons
Publishers Since 1838
200 Madison Avenue
New York, NY 10016
http://www.putnam.com/putnam

Copyright © 1996 by Bonni Goldberg

Library of Congress Cataloging-in-Publication Data
Goldberg, Bonni.
Room to write : daily invitations to a writer's life / Bonni Goldberg.
p.   cm.
"A Jeremy P. Tarcher/Putnam book."
Includes index.
ISBN 0-87477-825-5 (acid-free paper)
1. Authorship. I. Title.
PN 151.G55   1996   95-36134 CIP
808—dc20

Book design and illustrations by Judith Stagnitto Abbate
Cover design by Mauna Eichner
Cover illustration © by Geo Kendall

Printed in the United States of America
1   3   5   7   9   10   8   6   4   2
This book is printed on acid-free paper. ♾

For Geo,
who builds the desks
and gives me plenty of room

ACKNOWLEDGMENTS

Many people supported the creation of this book. I am grateful to Caroll Michels, Kay Hagan, Tim Wells, Jack Kammer, Rosemary Mahoney, and Joël Brenner for sharing their knowledge about turning ideas into books; my publisher, Jeremy Tarcher, and my editor, Robin Cantor-Cooke, for their vision and for treating me and this book with such integrity, care, and respect; my agent, Lisa Swayne, for being consistently enthusiastic and available; Carol Houck-Smith for her insights; Thérèse Murdza, Julie Convisser, and Natasha Sajé for reading and commenting on drafts of the manuscript; Steve Elkins for the office space; Linda Vlasak, Holly Best, Bob Brown, Sandra McKenzie, and Valerie and Juanita Leff for supporting my creative pursuits; Debra Tracey and Fran Stein for their unfailing belief in me; fellow writing teachers Ben Reynolds, Mary Fuller, and Jean McGarry; all of my teachers, especially Margaret Thaine, Adrienne Miller, Steve Diner, Grace Paley, Olufunmilayo Jomo, Jean Valentine, Kei Takei, and John Barth for their varied visions and combined passion; and all the folks I teach who keep me inspired.

Contents

INTRODUCTION

WHAT MAKES SOMEONE A WRITER? Writers write. Creative writers write *and* cultivate creativity. The urge to tell a story or shape a poem is a calling. To act on the urge is to answer that calling.

This book will help you write creatively, or if you already write—creatively or otherwise—it will serve as a companion if you are ready to develop and discover more about yourself as a writer. Within these pages you can explore your creativity while cultivating it. From each study you will learn about how you write and to trust your intuition. It is a process for those who believe that writing, like any creative endeavor, is a way of life, a way of understanding the world. Writing is being part of a lineage that embraces events, circumstances, landscapes, and people in ways that connect you to your spirit and our collective consciousness. This book will help you become accustomed to moving in and out of the places where writing happens.

It is called *Room to Write* because each page is a door into one of the places from which creative writing emerges: imagination, emotion, intellect, and soul. "Room to write" also refers to creating room for your writing by providing a way for you to begin each writing session and topics with which to start your writing process.

Writing, like any spiritual undertaking, has many paths, but only one direction—deeper. Whichever path you follow, a few fundamental rules apply:

1. The most important action you can take is to show up on the page;
2. The more you can give up control over what you write, the more genuine your writing will be;
3. Making room in your life to write generates even more room for your writing;

4. The only true obstacle to writing creatively is a lack of faith that appears as fear and self-judgment.

The book is divided into two hundred studies: you might try doing three or four each week. Having said that, it isn't at all necessary to follow this schedule. There is nothing magic about the order of the studies, either. Whether you do them chronologically, randomly, or by topic will tell you something about the way you write. Not whether it's good or bad, just something about how you work. If you pick studies randomly, perhaps you compose the same way. So you might not want to try and start your novel idea on page one. Instead you might be more productive beginning wherever you land. How much time you devote to any study is also up to you. We each have our own rhythm to consider, and there is no formula for success based on the length of time you allot a topic. Try writing until you have nothing more to say, then write at least one more paragraph or stanza.

Use these studies to begin journal entries, as warm-ups or sketches before getting down to "serious" writing, to mine ideas for a piece, to help develop characters for your novel by doing the studies as one of them, as prompts for your writing group or class, or to pass the time on a rainy Sunday night.

Sometimes I use the word *diving,* which is my term for what Natalie Goldberg calls writing practice, Deena Metzger calls automatic writing, and is often referred to as associative or free writing. Although these are the same activity, the emphasis differs. Try the first study, "Diving In." Diving is writing without stopping, crossing out or changing any words. The idea is to reach the uncensored material by letting go of the outcome and keeping the words flowing quickly. You are diving into your imagination. The only rule is, don't stop. You succeed as soon as you fill up the number of pages you allotted to the dive.

Many of the studies offer more than one way of approaching a topic. Let your intuition guide you. Whichever option is most enticing is the one to do. You may decide to try all the options at one sitting or each individually over time. The studies are designed to be reusable. No matter how you approach a study the first time, you will glean a new understanding the second time around. The quotes are furnishings to complement each study and further stir you.

No matter how successful you are at fine-finishing your writing or making it public, you must always return to that first process of sitting down to write and finding out what you have to say, the putting of words together through grappling with the thoughts, associations, emotions, and connections that form among your intellect, imagination, and heart. It is for this reason that I have gathered studies I use as a writer and creative writing teacher: to offer you a daily invitation to write and a way to enter the writing—a door for you to open. What you find behind each door is an adventure. Explore every room. Listen to yourself. Trust what you hear.

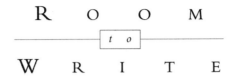

DIVING IN

DIVING IS A FORM of free writing. The word or phrase with which you begin is your jumping-off point. Once you write it, let it take you anywhere it wants to; follow it faster than the speed of understanding. You are descending through the waters of your mind, leaving logic and propriety behind for the sake of exploration.

It can be a challenge the first few times. You'll be tempted to come up for air (pause to reread what you've just written), adjust your gear (stop to fret over grammar, punctuation, and spelling), check your oxygen supply (censor what emerges). It takes practice to let go and trust the fluid world of your thoughts. When you encounter whale-sized emotions, let them float across the page like clouds as you continue to write. Whatever you do, don't stop writing.

Herman Melville understood the importance of the plunge. He, too, compared writers to divers: ". . . that whole corps of thought-divers, that have been diving and coming up again with bloodshot eyes since the world began." When you jump in and complete the descent, you emerge bleary-eyed and breathless. You have journeyed far.

TODAY dive into writing by choosing any one of the following words that have more than one meaning: bear, cleave, lie, sewer, tear, *or* desert. *Start by copying the word and quickly, without stopping for any reason, continue writing until you reach the end of the page. Making sense is unimportant. Your goals are speed and endurance. If you get stuck, repeat whatever word you've just written until something new spills out. After you finish read the result. Don't forget to breathe, and try not to tense up your hand. Ready, set, go . . .*

> I love all men who dive. Any fish can swim near
> the surface, but it takes a great whale to go down-
> stairs five miles or more.
> HERMAN MELVILLE

M E M O R Y   I S
I M A G I N A T I O N

MEMORY IS AN ASPECT of imagination. For writing, memory is one of your most important tools. But you don't need an excellent memory to use it well. A single phrase, an image, a fragment of a story, one object from the past is enough to spark the creative, intuitive mind. Especially rich are incidents and images stored away that you aren't sure ever actually occurred; dreams or stories someone has spoken of so many times that they're engraved as past realities. No matter what their source may be, memories are doorways to new pieces of writing.

Memory is like a muscle. The more you use it, the stronger it becomes. One memory sparks another. Each time you write from memory, another fragment filed in that ninety percent of the human brain that science doesn't understand slips into consciousness and a creative shift takes place.

BEGIN with the phrase "I remember" and start writing. It doesn't matter whether you stick with one memory or list several. You can retrieve memories from as far back as childhood (or past lives!) to as recently as yesterday. If you get stuck just keep repeating the phrase "I remember," in writing, until something else forms in your consciousness. Don't even be concerned with the authenticity of the memory. Just record whatever comes to you. Don't stop until you have filled two pages.

Memory is a net.
OLIVER WENDELL HOLMES, SR.

I D O N ' T R E M E M B E R

J UST AS EXERCISING A MUSCLE involves resistance, it strengthens the imaginative mind to approach it from an angle it resists. What you don't remember is also material for your imagination to build on. Non-memories may involve parts of the past you have difficulty recalling. They may include what has been absent from your life: *I don't remember having my own bedroom.* They might even be humorous or sarcastic: *I don't remember ordering a blizzard for the day I was supposed to fly to the Bahamas.*

This time, begin with the phrase, "I don't remember," and fill up a page. If you draw a blank at any point, repeat the phrase "I don't remember," in writing, until something else forms in your consciousness. Notice if one of these non-memories suggests a section of a piece, an experience for one of your characters, or perhaps a topic to write about. Notice what subjects of non-memories emerge: are they the same themes you often write about? If not, further explore one of the new ones.

Not knowing when the dawn will
come I open every door.
E M I L Y D I C K I N S O N

In the Beginning There Was the Word

You probably have a vivid and early memory of encountering words, spoken or written, that profoundly affected you. It might have been the first time you realized the neon sign over the convenience store had a meaning, or a word or phrase you learned and loved to repeat, or the first time you heard a foreign language, or an image you saw in your mind the first time you heard a compound word like *dragonfly* or *Iceland*. It was probably a private experience. It shook you. You might even have had a physical reaction; it was the beginning of your romance with words.

Today write about the first time words profoundly affected you. Describe the situation, what led up to it, the moment of the encounter, your physical reaction, and something else that was taking place in the same setting but had nothing to do with your experience. Feel free to allow your imagination to supply whichever of these elements you can't recall. You might try this as a poem.

> The words! I collected them in all
> shapes and sizes and hung them like
> bangles in my mind.
> Hortense Calisher

~~F A I L I N G~~

Y<small>OU MUST UNDERSTAND</small> that as long as you are writing there is no such thing as failing. THERE IS NO SUCH THING AS FAIL-ING! There is only learning. It is true that you may not produce what you intended to, or that you didn't achieve the impact you had hoped to achieve (yet), but this isn't failure. Writing is too fluid to categorize this way. Who's to say that a line, image, or idea from a piece nobody understood, or a piece with which you were never really satisfied, won't re-appear as a gem in a future work?

At the same time, you don't have to hold on to every line you've ever written. You will write a whole lot of junk along the way. That's good! Feel free to write as much junk as you like. It will help you to learn how to discern the fruit from the mulch, the shark's teeth from the broken seashells along the shore. And don't worry if you discard a passage or a line that might have been a treasure. You won't run out or run dry, at least not for very long. All writers have dull periods, but they don't last indefinitely unless you really work hard at cultivating them.

Writing isn't a test. You can't fail, and there are no wrong answers. You don't get punished for skipping out on your writing time; you get another day to make a little more progress.

T<small>ODAY</small> write a full page of junk. It can be trite, repetitive, vague, clunky, melo-dramatic, gibberish—the worst stuff you can muster. Read it over and notice all the elements you understand about writing through the intentional ways you wrote against them. Now crumple, tear, or delete the page and toss it in the trash along with your belief in failure.

Try again. Fail again. Fail better.
S<small>AMUEL</small> B<small>ECKETT</small>

S N O T

THERE ARE MANY SUBJECTS you may think of as naughty, impolite, or simply inappropriate to write about even though they are universal experiences. These are not the dark subjects like incest or abuse, but the unmentionables, the ones you would never bring up in polite company, the social taboos, like belching. The great fifteenth-century Zen master Ikkyū wrote profound and wonderful poems that mentioned human feces. It is freeing to spend some time writing about such things because it helps you recognize and shift out of the subtler ways that you censor your writing. It can also be a lot of fun to write about what you think of as rude.

TODAY, for a minimum of one full page, write about snot. Afterward, consider how you felt before you began, as you wrote, and once you were finished. Record your responses. Check if any material emerged that you could incorporate into a piece you are working on. Or, list other unmentionable topics you could explore as you write.

You will do foolish things, but do them
with enthusiasm.
COLETTE

P I E C E   by   P I E C E

Y<small>OU WILL NOTICE</small> I use "pieces" to refer to writing. This is to emphasize that these studies relate to all types of creative writing. It is also to remind you that the process of creating includes staying open to whatever form best suits your material.

Just because you have always written stories doesn't mean that poetry or performance art won't come stumbling out. Most writers work in more than one form. Terms like short fiction, prose poem, and creative nonfiction attest to the organic nature of writing.

Grace Paley speaks of starting out as a poet and, feeling her poems weren't strong enough, going on to write fiction. If she had thrown up her hands and given up on writing because her poetry wasn't working, we would never have had the gift of her generous and beautiful stories. She also continues to write poems.

The creative mind is not organized into dispensers of poetry, novels, essays, and plays, siphoning off rations of material each in its turn. It's messier than that. A children's book comes up in the middle of a play; a stanza of a poem is taking up room in the second draft of an essay that you have to finish by two-thirty, and a line you wrote six years ago is sitting in your notebook undecided about what it wants to be.

*T*O*DAY start writing with no thought about what form the material will take. Or, select material you already have and try it out in another form. Pick from short story, poem, essay, performance monologue, creative nonfiction, children's story.*

> You know, you don't always have a
> choice of what you're going to write.
> You're not a cow that can give cream
> with one udder and milk with another.
> B<small>RUCE</small> D<small>UFFY</small>

ANOTHER PERSPECTIVE

YOU DON'T ALWAYS have to rack your brain to come up with an idea for a piece. Why not look at a well-known tale from the perspective of someone other than its protagonist? It's a way to recast the motivation behind an event or highlight subtle elements of a situation that become significant if you examine them. For instance, tell the story of Goldilocks and the Three Bears from the perspective of the Mother Bear who might have had a terrible morning before leaving the cottage, or had always longed for a daughter so when she saw the human girl asleep in her cub's bed a well of emotion rose in her heart.

Or what if the myth of Orpheus and Eurydice were related from the point of view of Eurydice instead of Orpheus? In the original, Eurydice gets lost in the forest and stumbles into the underworld, and Orpheus goes to Hades to try and get her back. What if Eurydice were having second thoughts about Orpheus and ran away on purpose? When Orpheus went down to the underworld to rescue her, was she glad to see him or did she sabotage his mission by calling his name so that he would turn around—the one action that would keep her from returning with him? A story told in another character's voice creates a new story.

TODAY choose a favorite biblical or literary story or a fable or fairytale. Pick another character who appears in the story and tell it through his or her eyes.

Creativity oscillates between what is
given and what can be discovered.
DEENA METZGER

MAKING CLAY

LAURIE'S SUPERVISOR WANTED her to write a grant proposal. She wanted some parameters: what should be emphasized, how the narrative portion should be ordered, what level of knowledge could be assumed of the proposal's readers. He told her to just write up something and show it to him. She couldn't write a word.

Make clay, I told her.

She had gotten ahead of herself. She wanted to sit down and write a grant proposal: to mold words into a complete structure, like a sculpture. But her boss was asking her to make the clay: to create the material from which the proposal would be formed.

You can't make the sculpture before you mix up the water and earth and make the clay. She started writing.

Sometimes the work of writing is making clay: creating material to select from and discard. This type of writing is intentionally messy.

To practice making clay, today start with the word game *and dive in for three pages. You don't have to write in complete sentences. When you are done, read over what you have written. Highlight any phrases or passages you like and save them for a poem or a scene in a story.*

Warning: You may not like anything you wrote. Don't let that stop you from trying this study several times over using different words. You will find gems in many of the pages you write this way, but never in every one. Trust me; if you continue to use this technique, you will find it invaluable.

> I might write four lines or I
> might write twenty. I subtract and I
> add until I really hit something. You
> don't always whittle down,
> sometimes you whittle up.
> GRACE PALEY

D E S T I N Y

Hᴀᴠᴇ ʏᴏᴜ ꜰᴇʟᴛ ᴛʜᴇ same way about destiny all your life, or has your view evolved? Destiny is one of the Big Subjects in writing. Whether or not you ever come right out and write specifically about it, your views about destiny will surface in your work. The question of whether our lives are ruled by fate or free will, or the balance between them, determines the responsibility our characters and narrators take for the outcomes of their actions. Think about your favorite stories. How does destiny figure into them?

Tᴏᴅᴀʏ, begin by copying the word destiny *in your own handwriting and see where it takes you for two pages. Or, record a dialogue between the characters in one or two of your pieces on their beliefs about destiny.*

> Our wills and fates do so contrary run
> That our devices still are overthrown;
> Our thoughts are ours, their ends none of our own.
> Wɪʟʟɪᴀᴍ Sʜᴀᴋᴇsᴘᴇᴀʀᴇ

WHAT A CHARACTER

WHAT'S THE FIRST THING you notice about a stranger who walks into the room? Describing people is a significant part of creative writing. It is advantageous to your descriptions if you're aware of what aspects of a person you pick up on first: physical appearance, personality, style of speech or clothing, habits, etc. Knowing what comes naturally in your character descriptions will remind you of which other characteristics to observe to round out your portraits of people.

PICK someone you know either intimately or superficially and see on a fairly regular basis. Describe this person. When you are finished, notice what you concentrated on first, what aspects you have included and what you have left out. Did you include a physical description but leave out the way this person talks? Spend another half page on an element of character that didn't appear in the original description, or rework the portrait by beginning with the last category of characteristics to show up in your original description.

I think what we do is take what *we*
understand of both ourselves and what
we see around us. Our own nature
makes a selection; it selects which
things please you more.
LOUISE NEVELSON

THE EYES OF THE BEHOLDER

JUST AS IMPORTANT AS being able to describe another person is the ability to see through her or his eyes. We have the habit of believing that our own perspective is the most compelling way of seeing things and sometimes we limit our writing to this one view.

Think about films and novels in which characters temporarily find themselves in someone else's body. The characters inevitably learn something important about who they are. This is also true while writing. Each time you step out of yourself you also discover parts of yourself. For instance, we each walk around with an image of who we are and how others experience us. But what would you notice if you could see yourself through someone else's eyes? This is a step toward extending your ability to portray character.

TODAY describe yourself through the eyes of the character that you chose to describe in the study preceding this one. If you didn't do the previous study, do it now, and then begin this one.

I have to make myself up every day.
SPALDING GRAY

CRITICAL MASS

A CRITICAL INNER VOICE taunts as you create. You can ignore it, try to reason with it, seek counseling, or embrace it. Each of us must learn to live with it if we are going to write. I don't know any creative artist who has been able to permanently silence this voice. The best that most of us can do is acknowledge it and keep writing anyway.

But because strong writing comes from all your faculties, it helps to look at the ways the voice may be *helping* you write, too. Even though what it says may make you doubt your skill and talent, each time you write in spite of it, your commitment to writing deepens. It's as if having to struggle past the doubt strengthens your conviction. The type of energy it takes to move past it actually taps into the creative process.

It's not exactly that you need to feel grateful for the internal critic; all of us would be delighted to grow as writers without it. But as with any presence as forceful as it is common, it's worth considering how it can be an enlightening force.

TODAY turn your internal critical voice into a character. What is its gender? How does it look? How does it smell? Who are its favorite writers, and why?

> Most of the methods of training the
> conscious side of the writer—the
> craftsman and the critic in him—are
> actually hostile to the good of the artist's side;
> and the converse of this proposition is like-
> wise true. But it is possible to train both sides
> of the character to work in harmony, and the
> first step in that education is to consider that
> you must teach yourself not as though you
> were one person, but two.
> DOROTHEA BRANDE

PRE-UNDERSTANDING

WRITING IS DISCOVERY. Much of what develops from deep-diving writing sessions is material that is ahead of our understanding. You may not comprehend a good deal of what comes out of you.

Writing ahead of yourself is one way creativity propels you. Your job becomes making sense of the enigmatic phrases and images you produce. Mysterious metaphors and similes that you conjure are one example. Through further writing sessions your awareness of their meaning takes shape intellectually or intuitively. Then you grasp something that you hadn't appreciated or noticed before and use it to deepen the piece.

At times you may even write something that later becomes a reality in your own or another's life. This is not a sign that you are psychic. It is a sign that you are tapping into the stream where imagination and intuition meet. Realizations that bubble from this place are reminders of the purpose of writing. When you experience something that you had previously written and then reread your words, the power of writing scintillates through your being.

TODAY choose a phrase, passage, metaphor, or simile that is perplexing to you that surfaced during a previous diving session. Copy it on a new sheet of paper and spend some more time with it. Use it in a dialogue; list your associations with it; choose a key word and create an acrostic from it (see p. 107); draw it; say it out loud several times changing your tone, pitch, or accent each time. Use whichever of these ways appeals to you to explore and learn from this mysterious gift you have given yourself.

Writing is like carrying a fetus.
EDNA O'BRIEN

WHAT YOUR NOSE KNOWS

I ONCE TOOK CARE of a stray dog for a week. I was struck by the way he used his nose to make his way through the unfamiliar streets. He would sniff indiscriminately: garbage, flowers, people, bugs.

My grandmother's house has a distinct odor that includes the onions and oregano she often cooks with. These smells linger in the air along with those from my grandfather's oil paints and the cleaner they use on the rugs. Occasionally, I will enter a café that has a similar smell and I will, for a moment, be transported to their house on Avenue L in Brooklyn.

It is said that before we even speak to others, we form impressions of them based on their scent. Odors have a powerful impact on us. Smells bring back vivid memories of people and places. There are odors that ignite passion and sensuality and others that repel. Our culture produces thousands of products that alter a person's scent or our surroundings.

When drinking wine, you're supposed to savor the bouquet before you partake of the flavor, as if the fragrance of the wine prepares you for its taste. Notice too, all the words I've used for smell: odor, scent, bouquet, fragrance.

DESCRIBE smells today. You can list significant smells, or describe a place or person using only your sense of smell. Let everything that comes from your imagination, emotions, or observations filter through your nose!

Smell is a potent wizard that transports
us across thousands of miles and all the
years we have lived.
HELEN KELLER

E A T   I T

ONE OF LIFE'S GREATEST pleasures is the ability to taste. Salty, sweet, nutty, sour, fruity, spicy, and on and on. What is your favorite food? Your comfort food? What do you refuse to eat? Taste is a delicious place to hone your descriptive skills. Describing flavors can be as simple as listing their ingredients or as complex as portraying the way different foods and spices relate to one another.

Even more enticing can be describing the way a person tastes. By this, I don't mean cannibalism, but rather the flavor of a person: their physical taste (such as when you kiss) or that of their personality. What flavor is your best friend? Your dog? What is your flavor?

TODAY write only through your sense of taste. Speculate on and imagine the taste of whatever surrounds you. Without necessarily writing about food, experience the world as flavors.

Savor them in your mouth, try them on
your typewriter.
RAY BRADBURY

L I S T E N   C l o s e l y

ALL WORDS ARE ASSOCIATED with sound. Writing is using words with their volume turned down. In poetry the volume is turned up a little bit higher due to the attention poets pay to rhythm, meter, and the music of the words. But whatever you write, don't ignore sound.

A piece isn't complete until you're satisfied with how it sounds out loud: the rhythm of the phrasing, the melody of the words grouped together. It is like choreographing a dance: each word is a member of the company and you are in charge of orchestrating their movements.

Are there words or phrases you like to say because they feel good to your ear and in your mouth? One of my favorite phrases to speak is the first line of a Coleridge poem, "In Xanadu did Kubla Khan a stately pleasure dome decree." I feel as if I have something wonderful in my mouth. It is the sounds of the words more than their meaning that pleasures. Listening to novels on tape, especially those with characters from cultures which have distinct rhythms in their speech, help you to tune in and absorb the nuances of sound.

TODAY write for sound: list words and phrases whose sounds you like or dislike; describe sounds around you; create a dialogue in which the rhythm of the speech emphasizes the tone and subject of the conversation. Whichever of these ways you choose to approach sound, pump up the volume.

> For certain engineering purposes, it is desirable to
> have as silent a situation as possible. Such a room is
> called an anechoic chamber . . . a room without
> echoes. I entered one . . . and heard two sounds . . .
> the high one was my nervous system in operation,
> the low one my blood circulation.
> J O H N   C A G E

D o ~~N o t~~ T o u c h

Howoften do you include texture in your descriptions? How thoroughly and deeply do you touch things? Does your beloved's skin feel only soft, or do the small hairs, spongy subcutaneous fat, taut muscle, and even knobby bone fill out the experience for your reader?

The impulse to touch or to want to touch something unusual or intriguing is natural. When shopping for clothes do you ever finger the fabrics of items you find repulsive and would never buy as well as those you're attracted to? If our socialization didn't discourage us from learning through our tactile sense we would stroke whatever makes us curious: other people's hair, sculptures, unidentifiable objects.

What is it that you learn from touch, from texture? Think of handshakes, hugs, the touching of rare or holy objects.

TODAY write through texture: list as many textures as you can think of; feel your way around a person, an object, an event; meditate (in words) on what you understand about objects or people through texture and touch.

Our skin is what stands between us and
the world.
D I A N E   A C K E R M A N

The "D" Word

WHENEVER I HEAR the word *discipline* I feel like someone is scratching fingernails along a chalkboard. I see whips. I get cranky. I am a compulsive, task-oriented soul more than a disciplined one. Still, there is no way around the fact that it takes a lot of the "d" word to write.

"Writers write, writers write," goes my mantra. I sit down and begin, or I stay in my seat until I have written one more page. This is the unglamorous side, the sometimes boring, dull, daily routine, the paperwork aspect of any job.

For some folks the word *commitment* works better. For me, *acceptance* is the image because it is from this perspective that I give up self-importance and return to the ordinary courage of doing what I have to do to complete another day's work. But I know a brilliant, successful writer whose drive to keep writing comes from competing with his father. Whatever works to keep us showing up. . . .

TODAY write about discipline. You might begin a poem or essay on what you have recently come to accept, or still refuse to accept in this area. Or, you can follow one of your characters through the process of dealing with an aspect of discipline. Or, recall an incident related to discipline from your past.

Finally, one just has to shut up, sit
down, and write.
NATALIE GOLDBERG

L I E S

EVERYONE LIES. WE'RE NOT supposed to, but we do anyway. All of us have lied in the past and we are likely to lie again in the future. Some people profit from their lies, while others get into trouble. Nobody likes to be lied to unless they themselves are hiding from the truth. The power derived from most lies is the ability to withhold, to trick someone else, to control reality. But lies aren't always bad. What was the last lie you are glad you told? Why was it a good lie?

What motivates a character to lie is often more telling than the lie itself. You can incorporate the lies that your characters speak more convincingly by beginning with your own motivations for lying.

TODAY write only lies. They can be absurd ones, such as, last night I had dinner with the President in Honolulu, or the lies you tell yourself and/or others. Without judgment, be a total liar. Or, write down lies you have told and, in retrospect, what motivated you to withhold the truth. Or, write a scene in which one of your characters considers telling a lie.

> The past is not only that which happened but also that which could have happened but did not.
> TESS GALLAGHER

W I S H F U L   T H I N K I N G

HOW MANY WISHES have you made? Can you even count every: birthday, first star, coin tossed into a fountain, exasperated, wistful, regretful utterance? Most of us wish all the time. The first poem I ever wrote was about wishes. I was ten years old.

Some wishes become familiar friends over the years. Others develop through time and circumstance. You probably didn't wish for three extra hours in the day until you were responsible for taking care of yourself and others.

Wishes are voices of the imagination, taking you out of the realm of reality on a daily basis. For this reason, in creative writing, it is worth paying attention to them.

TODAY record your wishes: the secret ones, the old favorites, or the one that is speaking to you right now.

What counts is what one wants to do,
and not what one does.
PABLO PICASSO

Dreams convene in our imaginations. One short-story writer I know gets all his material from his dreams. Another friend has begun a novel based on a recurring and ever expanding daydream that has kept her company on long plane rides, in traffic jams, and through several cycles of laundry.

Even if dreams aren't a source of material for your work, record them when they are particularly vivid. Your imagination is at play. Join the game. In the process of writing dreams down some parts become suddenly elusive and others may emerge that you had forgotten.

Dreams are supposed to intrigue us. They are a topic of science, psychology, spirituality, and literature: why we have them, how to interpret them, how to recall them more vividly, what they mean. If we don't dream we go insane. Each of us chooses ways to understand their purpose.

Today write down a dream. It can be a recurring dream, one from childhood, a daydream or a nightmare. As you write, notice which parts of the dream elude you and which parts become clearer. Feel free to fill in the blank spots, alter, elaborate on, or extend the dream sequence.

The kind of imagination I use in
writing, when I try to lose control
of consciousness, works very
much like dreams.
A m y   T a n

SAYING THE UNSAYABLE

IF YOU CAN say it, why write it? Some writers work almost exclusively from this perspective. When you can't find the words to communicate an idea, feeling, or experience but you are compelled to express it anyway, the unsayable is urging you forward. As Donald Hall suggests in his essay "The Unsayable Said," you are attempting to add "the secret (unsayable) room of feeling and tone to the sayable story." Often it is difficult to convey because you have strong or mixed emotions about the subject.

You may relate the unsayable by charging up the language you use. To describe the experience of riding a motorcycle, *compare* the vibration of the handle bars to another sensation it reminds you of; *juxtapose* the conflicting details of your thoughts and sensations; make the *rhythm* of your sentences echo that of zipping down the road. These ways of reworking language create an alchemy that transforms ordinary words into jewels that sparkle with the full complexity of experience.

TODAY choose a feeling, idea, or experience that you haven't been able to express to anyone no matter how hard or often you have tried. Use any of the techniques mentioned above to help you convey what you are after.

> The role of the writer is not to
> say what we can all say but what
> we are unable to say.
> ANAÏS NIN

U N S P O K E N E X C H A N G E

THERE ARE MOMENTS in life when you hold back the words you are thinking and search for a tactful approach. Later the unspoken words ring in your head for a few hours trying to have their say. In almost every relationship unspoken words remain between people. These words collect in the back of the mind, filed away, for who knows what, until you consider them from a writer's perspective.

Unload this file of what you wanted to say but didn't, onto the page. Examine the lines. If any are interesting, you're on your way into the next piece of writing. If not, you've made room for something new.

TODAY retrieve an unspoken exchange and have it out on the page. Pick an oldie but goodie like the argument with your sixth-grade teacher or your college roommate. What did you hold back, censor, edit, or delete back then? Say it now, along with the way that you imagine the other person would have responded. Then let the exchange continue.

Remembering the past gives power to
the present.
F A E M Y E N N E N G

O   G O D !

LIKE DESTINY, THE QUESTION of God comes up in creative writing. Don't skip or ignore this subject. The God of your understanding, its absence, or your ambiguity about it figures in your writing.

God is one of the Big Topics. Writers address it directly or subtly in their work. The poet Louise Glück won a Pulitzer Prize for *The Wild Iris,* a collection of poems which question, accuse, revere, and tempt the presence of this force. Today it's your turn.

TODAY address God. Go to the source and speak your mind whether you are addressing an absence, a fallacy, or even if you have no idea who or what you are addressing. Pay attention to the tone you take. Is it despairing, reverent, chummy, angry? Next, consciously experiment with writing about God in a different tone.

> Why indeed must "God" be a noun?
> Why not a verb—the most active and
> dynamic of all?
> MARY DALY

IT'S ONLY NATURAL

THE NATURAL WORLD is an unending source of inspiration and wisdom. For those living in an urban environment it can be a challenge even to notice nature insisting itself between skyscrapers and through cracks in the sidewalk cement, but it *is* there.

When talking about personality, we also refer to someone's nature. Nature has to do with essence. The word comes from the Latin *nasci,* meaning to be born. Nature is the way things are before being tampered with. So it is a force in the external environment and an aspect of a person's internal character.

TODAY write about an aspect of nature, either human or environmental, that intrigues you. Or, spend one page on both senses of nature and then connect the two.

There are unknown forces within
nature; when we give ourselves
wholly to her, without reserve, she
leads them to us; she shows us those
forms which our watching eyes do not
see, which our intelligence does not
understand or suspect.
AUGUSTE RODIN

S E E I N G   I S   B E L I E V I N G

You DON'T SEE WITH your eyes alone. You see with your instinct, your intuition, and your imagination. When a stranger approaches you on an otherwise deserted street you assess the situation by sizing up the person—drawing on the person's physical appearance—but also on your previous experience with strangers, your gut reaction, and a mental flash of possible scenarios. When writing, exercise your full range of vision as well.

TODAY look at something, anything, and see it fully. Use all three ways of seeing to describe this thing. Notice which way of seeing is most challenging for you and which comes more naturally.

The true mystery of the world is
the visible, not the invisible.
O S C A R   W I L D E

A B S E N C E A S P R E S E N C E

SOME WRITING BEGINS with a sense of absence, a void, a sense of something missing or hidden. This unseen inspiration can take the form of an object, a person, or a lack of understanding. What you don't see, literally and figuratively, can be what fascinates and motivates you.

Purposely avoiding something can have the effect of amplifying its importance, giving it greater power. When writing it is eye-opening to explore what you don't see or understand as well as what you do. Just as you see with your eyes, instinct, intuition, and imagination, you can neglect to see with these same faculties.

BEGIN by writing the phrase "I don't see," and follow blindly wherever it takes you.

> I believe in not quite knowing.
> A writer needs to be doubtful,
> questioning. I write out of
> curiousity and bewilderment.
> WILLIAM TREVOR

I f , T h e n : M a k i n g S e n s e

MAKING LOGICAL CONNECTIONS between cause and effect is just as important to creative writing as freeing up imagination. If Riley eats a pepperoni pizza, he's not a vegetarian. If Deb exercises, she feels better. If Hugo practices his dives, he will improve. When you are grounded in the logical, even obvious, connections between action and consequence, you are able to develop a more subtle, unique, or surreal sense of how events, ideas, and actions are related.

Part of writing is keeping tabs on the nuts and bolts, cause and effect relationships in a piece. This aspect of writing takes place between the waves of material that wash up on the page. It may not at first feel as exciting as raw creation, but it will equalize you and prepare you for the next creative surge.

TODAY try several if, then statements. Start with simple ones, such as, "If I do the laundry, then I will have clean socks," and spin out in whatever direction beckons. Notice how thinking and writing this way for a while sharpens or changes the way you make connections.

> Everything should be made as simple
> as possible, but not simpler.
> A L B E R T   E I N S T E I N

FIRE WORKS

FIRE ISN'T JUST LIGHT and heat. It's a hot topic for writing. Its flames burn with personal, cultural, and collective associations. Do you remember the first time you were burned? In some religions fire's intensity is a source of purification; in others it represents damnation, the sea of hell. In Greek mythology, fire was what Prometheus stole from the heavens and gave to humans in order to make them superior to all other animals. Tending a fire in writing stokes the heat of creativity through an element that has deeply impressed humanity from the beginning of time.

TODAY explore a personal story, memory, or belief about fire. Or start by writing the word fire, *and fill two pages without stopping.*

> When we lived closer to fire, when our
> lives depended upon the careful tending
> of the hearth, we had before us a symbol
> of the need for nourishment that lay
> deep in our souls.
> ANNE SCOTT

W A T E R   S O U R C E S

M ANY CULTURES CONSIDER water sacred. Our bodies are
ninety-seven percent water, so H_2O is a substantial part of each of us. It
is raining today: water dropping from the sky, gaseous clouds swelling
until they are so dense they transform and descend. Later the moisture
may change again—evaporate, rising back up into the atmosphere.

Water can symbolize transformation and purification, the unknown and potentially dangerous, even the cycle of time itself. How
does water speak to you?

*TODAY write about water: tap water, ocean water, rain water, any water or ex-
perience or dream of water that has both wet and whetted your imagination.*

> The cure for anything is salt water—
> sweat, tears, or the sea.
> I S A K   D I N E S E N

F E E D I N G   H U N G E R

Writing means admitting that you hunger. Each of us who spends time in the creative realm is hungry for understanding. Your characters also hunger, sometimes for the same food as you do and other times for different things.

Hunger is both a physical and an emotional experience. When desire becomes hunger, you can try to satisfy it, or you can encourage it. For example, if you long for the ocean, you might peruse ads for Caribbean vacations and rent videos with sensual beach scenes instead of driving to the nearest beach. Feeding hunger this way heightens your senses and your connection to what you hunger for; it opens a door to your deeper longing to capture it in written words.

TODAY write about what you hunger for. If this seems daunting, start with a simple desire, such as a craving for chocolate or sushi, and then move on to experiences that either feed or intensify your hunger.

One writes a novel in order to know
why one writes. It's the same with
life—you live not for some end, but in
order to know why you live.
A L B E R T O   M O R A V I A

A   QUESTION

Consider the following: a passage from Ecclesiastes, George Orwell's "modern English" translation, and a reconstruction of Orwell's translation from the Latin roots of the words he used. Which do you prefer?

1. I returned and saw under the sun, that the race is not to the swift, nor the battle to the strong, neither yet bread to the wise, nor yet riches to men of understanding, nor yet favor to men of skill . . .

2. Objective consideration of contemporary phenomena compels the conclusion that success or failure in competitive activities exhibits no tendency to be commensurate with innate capacity . . .

3. A truth strikes me and drives me to the place whence none of us escape: for we who, together, seek to ascend, whether we rise to the heights or slip, to fall from the lying rock, our paths are not measured to the size of what, from birth, our seeking hands could grasp and hold.

Whichever version you were most attracted to indicates your initial pleasure from reading and writing: rhythm, meaning, or imagery. The one you liked least is an aspect of writing for you to make special efforts toward.

TODAY write or rewrite a piece focusing on either rhythm, meaning, or imagery, depending on your preference. Or, write with your attention to whichever one is lowest on your preference list.

The first poems I knew were nursery rhymes, and before I could read them for myself I had come to love just the words of them; the words alone. What the words stood for, symbolized, or meant, was of very secondary importance.
DYLAN THOMAS

SAY IT WITH A KISS

KISSING USES ALL FIVE senses, which makes it an extremely sensuous act. It is a beginning and an end—the kiss hello and the kiss good-bye. There are a variety of romantic puckers (passionate, wet, teasing, rough, slow), as well as thrown-across-the-room kisses, tentative kisses, friendly pecks, and the reluctant ones that children give relatives or parents' friends. The poet Tess Gallagher's book *Portable Kisses* evokes a buffet of smooches.

Your first kiss is often etched in memory, and so is the solitary, experimental kind that you may have practiced on your arm, your pillow, or up against a mirror. Do you remember when you first found out French kissing involved touching tongues? I thought I would gag if I tried it, and I couldn't figure out how adults, who were forever concerned about germs, would willingly do something that seemed even more likely to spread a cold than drinking from someone else's soda bottle.

WRITE about kissing today. Besides being fun, it is an especially good practice for writing scenes between two people.

> We shelter under a warm net of
> kisses. We drink from the well of
> each other's mouth.
> DIANE ACKERMAN

You Are What You Wear

CLOTHING IS A PARADOX: it both covers and reveals a lot about us. It is a presentation that is meant to offset parts of our personalities. When you go to an important meeting you dress to look formidable, to make you feel solid when you speak.

Do you notice what other people wear? Think about the last person you saw. Can you recall something about her or his clothes? In how much detail? Perhaps you are less aware of the specifics of the clothing but have an impression of its style.

Writers often use characters' clothing to highlight aspects of their personalities. Who can forget the Wife of Bath in Chaucer's "Canterbury Tales"?

CONCENTRATE on clothes today. Take a character shopping on your page. Or, recall in detail clothing that you love or despise. Or, start with the word clothes *or* clothing *and see where it takes you. Or, write a short piece about a striking piece of clothing you have seen.*

His clothes and ring and shoes are all
going to talk . . .
ANNE LAMOTT

T W E N T Y   Y E A R S   L A T E R

T HE FUTURE IS an open field. You cannot conceive of it without using your imagination. You imagine it unfolding in various ways. These scenarios are variations on plot.

In one future you have your own talk show. In another you live by the sea writing books of poetry and novels. In another, you win the lottery and travel. In the nightmare version no one ever publishes a word you write and, despondent, you become an aimless wanderer muttering your plays in bus stations all night long.

Futurizing is good practice for developing plot. In the story "The Lady or the Tiger" we are left to imagine whether the princess will counsel her beloved to open the door that hides the tiger that will devour him or the one that reveals her handmaid who would become his wife. Either way, the story continues beyond the last word.

T ODAY choose one of your fantasies about what your life will be like twenty years from now. Develop a reasonable plot that would make the fantasy work out. Or do the same with a character you love from either a piece of your own or a favorite story.

But have the courage to write whatever
your dream is for yourself.
M AY   S ARTON

A T T I T U D E   A D J U S T I N G :
R E W R I T I N G

THE DREAM JOB DOESN'T come through. You have to make do where you are for an indefinite amount of time. You:

1. Arrive at work and the office looks shabby and anonymous. Or,
2. Arrive at work and head for the bulletin board that has a clever new cartoon tacked to it every Monday morning.

When an event unfolds differently than you were hoping you have the capacity to adjust your perspective.

A lot of writing is also readjusting your perspective: deciding what is worth keeping, finding the spot that has energy, or the one that is deadly dull and going back to make more of it.

Rewriting is as important as first thoughts. Every book that appears effortlessly written has gone through several rewrites. Including this one.

TODAY return to a piece that didn't gel and work more on it. Highlight the strong passages and copy one of them onto a new piece of paper. Write some more using the passage as a springboard.

> I've never quite believed that one
> chance is all I get. Writing is my
> way of making other chances.
> A N N E   T Y L E R

EVERYTHING AND THE KITCHEN SINK

A LOT MORE HAPPENS in a kitchen than making meals. When someone says, "Can I see you in the kitchen?" something pointed is about to take place. People tend to gather in the kitchen at parties. Kitchens are warm and inviting. They are also full of potentially dangerous objects: knives, shredders, burning-hot surfaces.

Some kitchens are battlegrounds in the war against germs. Those who live on take-out food view their kitchens as more of a decorative, nostalgic feature, like a fireplace that doesn't work.

Your kitchen is a symbolic place. Regardless of how much food is in your refrigerator or how many gadgets are in your cupboards, it is well stocked with associations, memories, and metaphors.

WRITE about your kitchen as if you were a detective. What has just taken place? Look for clues and contradictions. What lurks in the kitchen? Is it friend or foe? How does your kitchen reflect you?

Secrets simmer. Deals are cut.
Recipes are altered, stirred up.
Something is cooking . . .
ready, waiting, calling us home.
B. G. FROM "KITCHEN"

As You Like It

COMPARISON IS AS NATURAL as breathing. You hear a train and it reminds you of the ocean. You caress bark and remember your grandfather's knees. You look at tributaries and see your veins. One landscape melts into another. It's as if each time you encounter something it is imprinted over all the impressions that came before it; each impression is transparent.

The connection between two things can be obvious or subtle. Sometimes it's physical. Other times the similarity is experiential or has to do with function. The tendency to compare has to do with the interrelated nature of the universe we live in. It is possible to find some similarity between any two things. Babies and garbage trucks share similarities: they are both often smelly, move on all fours, and consume a lot. Trees and elephants both have trunks, have rough outer skins, live a long time.

TODAY draw comparisons between two things. Choose at least one from your surroundings. The other can be an object, a person, or an abstract concept like love, jealousy, fate. How many ways can you compare them? Go for at least twenty-five. Stretch yourself.

All things were together. Then mind
came and arranged them.
ANAXAGORAS

D E A R   A B B Y

WITHIN EACH OF US is the collective wisdom of our species. You can gain access to it through the act of writing. Your writing is moving when the reader recognizes a truth that resonates deeply. We read and write as often as a way to remember as to learn.

Writing novels, stories, and dramatic monologues calls on us to hear the voices of reason, passion, advice, and concern conversing inside us all the time. It isn't that we need a quiet place to work so intently we won't be distracted, but that we need quiet to concentrate on listening to one voice at a time. Each voice from our collective wisdom is also the kernel of a character developing.

TODAY choose a situation in your life about which you need advice. Start by presenting the problem. Listen to the different internal voices that respond. Then home in on one voice at a time and transcribe the advice verbatim. Use one or more of these voices to develop characters.

Nobody can give you wiser advice
than yourself.
CICERO

C H A I N - C H A I N - C H A I N

SOMETIMES THE ONLY WAY through the gate of creativity is trickery. There are days the mind is blank and nothing seems important enough to write about, or everything feels too large to approach. Sometimes you just forget how to write.

It is in these moments that you might rifle through the poems, stories, and essays you've written and wonder, How did I do that?

Don't give up at this point and do the laundry. Instead, become playful, stop taking yourself so seriously, and when the resistance loosens its grip, slip through the gate.

TODAY try a trick. Write one of the following words at the top of the page: fence, road, boil, or fall. Now without thinking or stopping, write whatever other words come to mind in a list down the middle of the page until you reach the bottom. Write a piece in which each line uses one of these words in the order in which they appear.

> I fool myself, in a good way, into dodg-
> ing the pressure. I tell myself that I'm
> not trying to write a scene, I'm just
> making some notes for the day . . .
> MARSHA NORMAN

B E A F R A I D , B E V E R Y A F R A I D

FEARS ARE GREAT motivators, especially for writers. Much of our strongest material comes from what we are afraid of. When you call up your fears in ritual or prayer you also call up protective forces. It is the same with writing. In fact, the act of writing is what protects you. It's like homeopathic medicine. You take small doses of your fears in combination with written words and they create a kind of antibody: a cathartic human experience that authenticates your strength and fragility.

MAKE a list of the things you fear. Pick one and describe it in concrete and specific detail.

> What I fear in writing is the
> safe decision.
> A N N E R I C E

P R O T E C T I O N

WRITING IS A COURAGEOUS act. Committing words to paper leaves you open to the inner workings of your soul, thoughts, and emotions. You invite the force of our human condition and its impact, no holds barred.

But in regular life you have an array of protective resources. As you observe people you will notice the defenses they use to filter out or avoid what is threatening; gestures, body language, facial expressions, and humor are some of the obvious ones.

It is natural to develop protections and use them. But as a writer you need to take a deep breath and submit to the white heat of experience.

TODAY make a list of the protections you use in life. Do you use them in writing, too? They may become some of the ways your characters protect themselves. Give one of your protections to a character and allow it to influence the plot and action. Or, write without your protections; for instance, without a time or page limit, in an environment you perceive as unsuitable, with a different writing implement than you usually use.

You must be unintimidated by your
own thoughts . . .
NIKKI GIOVANNI

WITH OR WITHOUT WINGS

HOW DO YOU FLY? Do you race cars, ride horses, parasail, take off on the page, lift weights, become airborne as you watch the gulls maneuver currents of wind, or do you get in an airplane and let the pilot take you away?

Flying is a great symbol. It has to do with reaching heights physically, emotionally, and spiritually. It has to do with taking off, ascending, soaring. The sensation of flying is an ancient metaphor for many experiences. Before we ever had ways to reach the sky, flying was a central image in literature.

As writers, when we take part in the traditions of our craft we start to soar.

WRITE about flying. How do you fly? Describe the feeling. Where do you go? Or, start by writing the word flying *or* wings *at the top of a piece of paper and see where it takes you.*

Every artist joins a conversation
that's been going on for generations,
even millennia, before he or
she joins the scene.
JOHN BARTH

I N S I D E   O U T

Go inside a stone,
that would be my way
C H A R L E S   S I M I C

W E DON'T LIVE and write according to the same physical laws. The poet Charles Simic enters a stone and we follow. But there are still rules in writing. An important one is that no matter how fantastic the event on the page, it must be emotionally real and probable in the reader's mind.

The best science fiction, horror, and fantasy writers create believable characters, plots, and outcomes. This is how they engage their readers and persuade them to travel to strange and unlikely places.

DESCRIBE *a place impossible to enter: the center of an erupting volcano, the fifth dimension. Turn the experience inside out. Let your imagination float and then anchor it to what is feasible.*

CURRENT EVENTS

Each of us is sparked by something different. It can be an image, idea, character, belief, subject, or theme. As we write, we come back to it again and again because it causes us to well up inside. The welling isn't always a good feeling. It can shock us to point out its importance and urgency.

I have two distinct experiences of what inspires me. One is a series of jolts; I write for a while and feel so overwhelmed that I have to stop and literally walk away from the work. Then it is difficult, even frightening, to return. But I am as drawn as I am repelled.

The second experience is that the words and ideas come faster than I can write them down. I'm chasing a runaway train. I have to rely on the wind to carry the momentum of what is flowing through me.

WHAT is one of your electric topics? Follow its current, wherever it takes you. Let your obsession power another piece. When you are done, read what you have written and ask yourself, what is illuminated?

I believe talent is like electricity. We
don't understand electricity. We use it.
You can plug into it and light up a
lamp, keep a heart pump going, light
a cathedral, or you can electrocute a
person with it. Electricity will do all
that. It makes no judgment. I think
talent is like that. I believe every
person is born with talent.
MAYA ANGELOU

N A T U R A L   R H Y T H M

W E SPEAK, WALK, AND write in rhythms. Our speech and gait developed as we imitated the adults around us. The rhythms in our writing have more mysterious origins.

For some, rhythm imitates the measure of words they can speak in one breath. For others it mimics a recurring sound in the landscape: ocean waves, subway trains, lawn mowers. Many of our rhythms echo the prayers and incantations of religious ceremonies or the cadence of the voice of someone dear to us.

Do you tend to write in long or short sentences? What type of dance or music would complement the beat of your words—waltz, blues, two-step, reggae, salsa?

It is impossible to predict where your sense of rhythm will come from, but by listening to your writing you can discover and hone your rhythmic patterns. You can also begin to consciously experiment with new ones.

READ some of your writing aloud. Read it more than once. Listen for the rhythm. What do you hear? Today write conscious of rhythm. Let it lead you. You can allow rhythm to drive action or plot. You can rework a piece to make the rhythm stronger, or you can experiment and change it.

> In the beginning was noise. And
> noise begat rhythm. And rhythm
> begat everything else.
> M I C K E Y   H A R T

1 0 1

As WRITERS, WE ARE often surprised by ideas and images we generate. Where do they come from? Sometimes it is divine inspiration. Other times it is from the deep well of memory.

Attempting to reach those waters can be frustrating. Or it can be fun. You can't command memory or inspiration to surface but you can reach out to them. Stretch your arms toward the well. Extend yourself.

By reaching toward material you move below the surface and discover the spring.

TODAY stretch your memory by making a list of "101 Places I've Been" or "101 Ways to Dance." Number your lines ahead of time. Generate the list as quickly as you can; try for fifteen minutes. Write whatever comes to mind even if it doesn't make sense. Don't quit until you have 101. What surfaced on your list that surprised you? Explore it.

> The pages are still blank, but there is a
> miraculous feeling of the words being
> there, written in invisible ink and
> clamoring to become visible.
> VLADIMIR NABOKOV

Aʀᴇ ʏᴏᴜ sᴜʀᴇ you want another piece of pie?" This sentence is
constructed as a question, but it isn't really an inquiry. It's an opinion: I
don't think you should eat any more pie.

In conversation, as in writing, a lot goes on between the lines: in-
sinuation, ulterior motive, innuendo. In writing, conversation is fertile
ground for developing character, conflict, and building suspense for just
this reason. In *Play It As It Lays,* Joan Didion's characters say more in the
pauses than the words:

> "I'm sorry."
> "I know you're sorry. I'm sorry."
> "We could try," one or the other would say after awhile.
> "We've already tried," the other would say.

A dialogue between characters can speed up a reader's heart,
quicken the breath. Think about the last conversation you had. What
was said between the lines? What was implied? Do you recall your physical sensations during the interaction?

*Wʀɪᴛᴇ dialogue that reveals more between the lines than what is actually being
said. See how much characterization or conflict you can develop solely through dialogue while still keeping the conversation believable. Or, begin with a talk
you've had recently and continue it in writing, keeping character development in
mind.*

It's not the answer that enlightens,
but the question.
Eᴜɢᴇɴᴇ Iᴏɴᴇsᴄᴏ

H IS MOOD IS AS changeable as the weather." A cliché, but one worth considering. When a human being embodies an idea or a quality it is called personification: King Arthur personifies nobility. The reverse of this, attributing human qualities to what is not human, is called anthropomorphism: the tree wept.

TODAY consider what type of weather corresponds to you right now: snow, lightning, rain, fog. How far can you take the comparison: mood, thought pattern, appearance, what you like to do for fun . . . ?

We are shaped and fashioned
by what we love.
J O H A N N   W O L F G A N G   V O N   G O E T H E

T Y P E   C A S T I N G

W HEN EXPLORING A confrontational or unpleasant subject, sometimes writers touch the reader deeply by approaching the subject indirectly. Humor and metaphor are the most effective means. These techniques give the reader a role in recognizing the message; it is a respectful approach.

In *Animal Farm,* George Orwell satirizes human society by comparing its various groups to animal species found on farms. This makes his scathing social commentary more powerful because even though we know the animals represent us, the distance created by the representation allows us to drop our defenses and get the meaning.

TODAY examine a group. It can be your co-workers, your characters, your family, any group. Then pick a category: vegetables, gardening tools, types of cereals, holidays, any category that comes to mind. Develop character sketches for each member of the group based on elements within your chosen category. For instance, if you choose vegetables as a category, write about what type of vegetable your main character looks like or acts like and why.

Transforming is not lying.
R A I N E R   M A R I A   R I L K E

You're Such an Animal

EXPLORING THE EXPERIENCE of other creatures challenges your observational skills.

In *The Hidden Life of Dogs,* Elizabeth Marshall Thomas observes and comments on the behavior of her canines. In this book of creative nonfiction, each dog is a character in a narrative drama complete with conflict, plot, climax, and resolution. Her goal is to say something about the nature of a species by remaining a detached observer.

But what would happen if she took one step closer? In other words, how would your observations of a dog (or cat, fish, or armadillo) translate into your imagined experience of being the animal? Would you still think in the human way you do? Notice the same things? Love the same creatures?

TODAY you're an animal. Choose one you have had some experience observing and interacting with. Or, write from the point of view of the animal with whom you identify most.

An animal's eyes have the power to
speak a great language.
MARTIN BUBER

T V

TELEVISION IS A HUGE influence in our culture. If you don't own one, most people consider you peculiar. Our imaginative consciousness is full of characters and personalities from the little screen. As a society we identify with these figures more than we do with our politicians, spiritual leaders, or artists.

Television is a force. It has great symbolic potential in literature. Whatever our opinions of and feelings about television, as writers we mustn't simply ignore it. This would be like ignoring the influence of nuclear power or telephones.

It isn't as if these inventions need to always appear in your work, but you should be aware of their influence as you write. How does one of your characters use the television? Is it on all day? Does she hate it, mute the commercials, watch only news?

BRING television or the influence of television into your writing today. Or, begin with the word television *and see what images, memories, and associations reveal themselves.*

> Why go to the trouble of constructing
> fantasies when a flick of the dial will
> produce them ready-made?
> ROBERT SOMMER

WHAT A JOKE

ARE YOU ONE OF those naturally funny people who is quick with one-liners and clever comebacks, or do you have to work at it? Humor has impact. It is the way the most people are most willing to approach the painful, ugly, and difficult parts of life.

Writing humorously is even harder than being funny in person. Some of us are blessed with this gift. The rest of us have to work at it. It is time well spent.

Fortunately, there are several types of humor to choose from: satire, irony, sarcasm, burlesque, parody, travesty, black comedy, and the list goes on. It is likely that the kind of humor you most enjoy will be the kind you will be most motivated to develop.

TODAY write down all the jokes and one-liners you can remember, then your favorite comedians. Notice the type of humor that most appeals to you. Or, write something that you think is funny; it may be an experience you had or something you observed. Look it over and imagine what your favorite comedian might do to the piece to make it funnier.

In order to nurture our creativity,
we require a sense of festivity, even
humor: "Art. That's somebody
my sister used to date."
JULIA CAMERON

W R I T E   O U T   L O U D

YOUR SPEAKING VOICE is one of your best teachers. The first and final revision technique for any type of creative writing is to read the piece out loud. I've attended fiction and poetry readings where writers read from new work with a pencil in hand, making changes as they go. While it's distracting to me as an audience member, as a writer, I understand. When I read a piece to others for the first time, I experience it with new ears. I can hear where it falters or loses momentum more objectively than I can reading silently to myself at my desk.

It helps to read a piece to at least one other person before sharing it with an audience, but even reading it aloud to yourself helps you to identify the weak spots. If you trip over a word or phrase, mark it and rework it later. When you read the piece to yourself, use your full voice and get out of your chair. It is done when you can read it standing on two feet without faltering.

TODAY read aloud twice a piece you have completed. If you have a tape recorder, tape yourself reading once and play it back. Either way, listen to yourself, paying attention to the sections that are awkward to speak as well as the ones that are confusing to hear. Mark these sections and rework them. Use the out-loud test to decide when the revisions are complete.

The voice is a second face.
GÉRARD BAUËR

R E C I P E S

Y OU WANT TO WRITE about love, destiny, evil, beauty, and a host of other abstract concepts. You look to writing teachers and astute readers. They tell you to start from the small, specific, concrete details and the big ideas will appear like the silhouette of a figure behind drawn shades. They are right.

But it isn't always possible to start from the small and work into the bigger picture. Sometimes you need to start very big and work your way down into the textures, smells, corners.

It is this way with cooking. You begin with a general idea of what you want to eat and then get down to the specific ingredients and preparation.

TODAY pick an abstract concept like truth, beauty, evil, *or* love. *Create a recipe. Start with a list of ingredients and then write about preparation. Don't forget to mention how many people the dish will serve and what else goes with it.*

Each era has its own recipe.
G E O R G E S   B R A Q U E

M A M A   M I A !

Have you ever wanted to trade in your mother? Every character has one. What would it have been like to be Caesar's mom, or Blanche and Stella DuBois's? This is a step away from using your personal life for all your material. A student of mine worked on this study and expanded it into a one-act play. Motherhood had momentum for her and became the subject for several short stories and poems.

Or maybe you feel you could write a whole volume on your own mother. She is half your gene pool, your first source of nourishment. Go ahead. Get it out. If you don't, she will make an appearance in all the older women you create; you know how mothers can be.

Today, in some way, write about your views of motherhood. Pick a well-known figure like Mae West or Marie Curie and describe what it might be like to be her child. Use first person to describe your impressions, or narrate a particular anecdote in third person. Or, write about your own mother.

> Everyone has several mothers, and they
> don't all die at the same time.
> Michael Ventura

RITUALS

WRITING IS A RITUAL. Not only the process but how the result (the story, the poem, the monologue) is received. You formalize—put into a form—whatever you write about. It is captured and contained outside of daily experience so that you can concentrate on it and encounter its deeper resonance.

This is the function of any ritual, to focus deeply in a place that has been prepared for such contemplation. When you enter your writing space it is like entering a place of worship. The perpetual motion of life is left outside.

The same is true when you read or listen to writing. The laundry, the carburetor, the weather, the credit card bill recede as you open the book or the recitation begins. The act of binding life in words is influential. It is an aspect of what Edward Bulwer-Lytton understood when he said the pen is mightier than the sword.

As you write about an experience today, be aware of formalizing, of containing the experience through the act of writing about it. Or, write about a ritual in which you have participated.

The aim of every artist is to arrest motion, which is life, by artificial means.
WILLIAM FAULKNER

Those rituals of getting ready to write produce a kind of trance state.
JOHN BARTH

OUR FATHER

FATHER ISN'T ONLY the man who gave you half your genes. Father is a powerful idea. Father is a degree of influence. Priests are referred to by this term. Sometimes God is too. In some cultures a member of the community, male or female, who is past a certain age or holds a special responsibility in the community is called father.

What your father imparts to you leaves an impression that shapes the way you take action. What kind of message did you get from your father about writing? If he doesn't know you write there is a message in that as well.

In *The Father,* Sharon Olds explores her relationship with her dying father. The title suggests that this sequence of poems portrays more than her particular father. She probes the role of father in a person's life and the degree of his force.

TODAY explore father. It can be your own or a character's. Or list images, memories, associations, and ideas about this role. In any way you choose, invoke father.

> It doesn't matter who my father was; it
> matters who I remember he was.
> ANNE SEXTON

TO GRANDMOTHER'S HOUSE

GRANDPARENTS. THEY ARE THE elders of your clan. Dead or alive, they are the focal point of stories about where you come from, who you are, what you are supposed to do.

I often begin a workshop with a timed writing study that starts with copying down the word *grandmother* or *grandfather*. Even folks whose grandparents died long before they were born write without stopping the whole time.

Sometimes they will opt to write about the grandparents they wish they had. This too is a source of history and origins, for longings are as much a part of your clan as the sequence of events that led you to where you are today.

Grandparents are a doorway to a cache of material. Once inside, blow away the dust of time and find the treasures in all the corners of the room.

TODAY begin with the word grandmother *or* grandfather *and let the memories and associations serve as tour guide. Examine what surfaces. Is it mostly character description, story, history, opinion, something else? Find a character, story, or poem to write.*

> I have a sense of these buried lives
> striving to come out through me to
> express themselves.
> MARGE PIERCY

WHO WAS THAT STRANGER?

WE ENCOUNTER STRANGERS each day: in the grocery store, at the office, in restaurants, on the bus. Yet only some of them catch our attention and fewer our fascination.

We are first struck by physical attributes. It can be a person's voice or eyes or clothing. But most of the time what holds our attention has to do with attitude, presence, and energy. All these terms refer to a person's spirit or soul.

Writers use physical traits to reflect aspects of a character's intangible qualities, such as personality and spirit. By ruminating about a character's spirit first, the physical description becomes an extension of his or her soul.

TODAY pick a stranger who fascinates you. First, describe the person's spirit, soul, or energy without relying on physical appearance. Then begin the physical description.

> I feel at times that I'm making up these
> little people and I've lost my mind.
> CAROLYN CHUTE

B O D Y   T A L K

CHARACTERS CAN DEVELOP from the most unlikely sources, especially if you become attuned to the more unusual places they can appear. For those who see conscious life in the vegetal and mineral world, characters may be based on trees or rocks; in fact, central characters may actually be trees and rocks.

For the rest of us, it takes an act of imagination to recognize the cast of characters in the subtler world.

Start this process in familiar territory; take your body, for example. You have unique relationships to certain parts: you love your shoulders, hate your legs, work with your upper arms, worry over your hair. Do you ever talk to them? "Looking good!" "Are you better today!" "Don't let me down now." Do they ever talk back?

Let them today.

CHOOSE a body part that receives a good deal of your attention. Begin a dialogue. Write something to the body part in script and on the next line, in print, let the body part respond. What kind of character is developing: feisty, apologetic, disillusioned? What story does this character have to tell? What has it learned from or taught you?

Censor the body and you censor breath
and speech at the same time.
HÉLÈNE CIXOUS

N o t   A l w a y s

THERE ARE WORDS that instructors and mentors counsel you to remove from your writing and from your thinking. One of them is *always*.

There is no such thing as *always*. It is an imprecise term. It is the nature of things to change. The sun will not always rise and the moon will not always orbit the earth. However, *always* does express a feeling associated with various people, events, and situations that evoke a sense of timelessness for us.

That timeless feeling can range from desirable to unbearable. Wherever it falls, it is better expressed through tone, details, and symbols than by the catchall *always* which is shorthand and short-changes your reader.

As you revise your work, go back to the places this word appears and exchange it for the real thing.

TODAY break the always *rule and get it out of your system once and for all. Make as many* always *statements as you can. Examine your statements. Are they mostly sentimental, sarcastic, complaining? This is where you are likely to find them in your writing.*

> Creative minds have always been
> known to survive any kind of
> bad training.
> A N N A   F R E U D

PICTURE THIS

JOHN GARDNER GAVE his writing students this assignment: describe a barn. The next week everyone had to read his or her description aloud. All the descriptions included similar details.

I've given the same assignment with the same results, even when each person swears to have described an actual barn they knew. In every description the barn had some combination of webs, rusting tools, a musty smell, a type of rodent or bird, a broken window, hay, shadows, a pail, peeling paint.

That's when the group discusses how writers have to write the expected, the boring, and the clichéd to reach the genuine material. Then we all sigh with relief and realize that the first version of a piece is bound to include some awful stuff.

TODAY describe a setting you know well or are now in the midst of. Write the most cliché-ridden, predictable, boring description that you can. No holds are barred. Go for the worst schlock you can imagine for one or two paragraphs. With that out of the way, begin again and write on a deeper level.

My object is to show what I have
found, not what I am looking for.
PABLO PICASSO

A N I M A L   S P I R I T

JENNIFER IS A painter. She is also a lion. She's happiest either napping or painting. If you disturb her nap she's grumpy, and if you disturb her painting time she will turn on you. When she goes on an excursion to New York or Washington, D.C., to view art, she becomes entirely focused on her purpose. She scans a gallery and stands in wait off to the side until she has a painting all to herself. Nothing and nobody intimidates her.

Kurt is a poet. He is also a spider. He spins intricate and beautiful poetry that holds you in its web. He is always writing and rewriting. He is purposeful and careful in all his actions from cooking to driving.

WHAT kind of animal are you? What qualities does that animal embody that you identify with temperamentally? Describe yourself as this creature. How does being this animal affect the way you write?

What can we writers learn from lizards,
lift from birds?
RAY BRADBURY

Point of View, Another

We are so immersed in our own language that we don't notice how it defines our point of view. There is no single word in English that corresponds to the Italian *viltà*, which means moral cowardice. In the Dagara culture the closest word they have to supernatural is the concept of *Yielbongura*, "the thing that knowledge can't eat."

The meaning of words in a language isn't the only aspect of it that creates a mindset about reality. The way a language is structured also reflects a particular point of view. The grammar and syntax of languages are constructions that house systems of thought.

e. e. cummings was one of the great English-language poets to disrupt syntax and grammar. When he wrote, "—but if a look should april me," he didn't just use April as a verb, he communicated the way a look can be a season by manipulating the parts of speech.

There are many ways to understand the world. This knowledge asks you to play with and challenge the limits of your language in order to glimpse other perspectives.

Today challenge your language. Write without conforming to syntax and grammar as you know it. Or, using a piece you've already written, disrupt the syntax and grammar. Or, make up a word that means something there is no single word for in your language, such as overwhelmed by technology. Write a definition of your new word and include it in a piece.

> Even though stories abound in my culture, we have no word for fiction. The only way I could get across . . . the Western concept of fiction was to associate fiction with telling lies.
> MALIDOMA PATRICE SOMÉ

IN DETAIL

DETAIL IS ELECTRIC. As a writing teacher I write "more detail" in the margins of people's work more often than any other phrase. In writing, detail is everything. It shocks, explodes, illuminates. It electrifies the reader's imagination and sparks a chain reaction of associations. Consider the differences between these sentences:

The restaurant was dingy. She sipped her espresso.
Her elbows felt greasy on the wobbly table. She sipped her espresso from a graying porcelain cup.

Through detail you can also dictate the pace of a passage by slowing down or speeding up the interval between two actions. And detail creates tone:

He wore the worn oriental rug around his shoulders as he stood across the street watching the fire die.

TODAY focus on detail. Be exhaustive in your detailing of something ordinary, like a teaspoon, in front of you; use at least twenty details. Go back over what you have written and pick out the electric ones. Now rewire your description for pacing or tone.

> I'm trying to cause people to be interested in the particulars of their lives because I think that's one thing literature can do for us. It can say to us: pay attention. Pay closer attention. Pay stricter attention to what you say to your son.
> RICHARD FORD

STRANGER THAN FICTION

TRUTH *IS* STRANGER than fiction. Our imaginations, though powerful, are not nearly as capable of creating as many variables as reality is. Writing imposes an order on events that isn't as evident or inevitable in our day-to-day lives. This is why writing is an art. This is also why it is often difficult to write about the goings-on in the world around us; it can feel impossible to attempt to make sense (sentences) out of the chaos.

You mustn't stop trying.

Something outrageous, unbelievable, unthinkable has already happened today. It will be something else tomorrow, and next month, and next year. You can count on it. Turn on the news, pick up a newspaper. It is your responsibility as a writer to tackle these goings-ons. It will not be easy. You may judge yourself not very good at it. That's okay. With time and practice you will learn how.

PICK an item from the news that troubles you. Write about it. You might start with straightforward opinion and reaction. You may have a character respond to the event or be pushed toward a decision because of it. You can retell the item in your own words, or the words of someone affected or involved.

Our job is to find a voice for
our own age.
NIKKI GIOVANNI

M E ,   M Y S E L F ,   A N D   I

S OONER OR LATER an artist makes self-portraits. The self is a perfect subject because we know ourselves better than anyone else does;
yet we have huge blind spots about our behavior that surprise and fasci-
nate us.

The self is also many-faceted. When you write about yourself
you can do it thirty times and not come up with the same portrait
twice.

It is said that artists are always, in some way, re-creating themselves in their work. There is truth to this statement; the act of creating
demands intimacy with various aspects of our humanity. Powerful writing makes the reader feel that same intimacy with the human condition
and less alone in the face of it.

*TODAY describe yourself: Fill a whole page with you. Notice which aspect you
concentrate on: physical appearance, emotional state, spiritual condition. Write
some notes on how this aspect speaks to something all of us feel. Or, write three
single-paragraph self-portraits that are completely accurate and totally different.
Title them "Me," "Myself," and "I." Or, describe an aspect of yourself that
mystifies you.*

I is another.
A R T H U R   R I M B A U D

THE FIRST TIME

THE FIRST TIME is memorable. When experiencing the new, our senses and emotions flood. We are shocked. We get a rush, sometimes delightful and other times traumatic.

During firsts we exist completely in the moment, without past or future flavoring the experience. We are open. We are new.

Our writing is fresh when we approach it from the position of firstness. This requires an act of imagination. It takes preparation. You may close your eyes and then open them on a familiar scene. You may pretend to be someone else meeting your brother for the first time. You might want to walk out of the room, close the door behind you and then reenter. Experiment with several ways to prepare yourself to write from this place of firstness.

TODAY write as if you are experiencing your subject for the first time, like it is your first encounter. Or, describe a character experiencing something for the first time. Or, start with the phrase "the first time," and write without stopping until you fill the page.

It is the first shower that wets.
ITALIAN PROVERB

O   B R O T H E R ,   S I S T E R !

W HO ARE YOUR BROTHERS and sisters? The terms brother and sister have many meanings. They may refer to your parents' other children, folks with a strong emotional connection, folks who share an ideology, culture, or spiritual community.

The relationships we label this way are often explored in writing. They are connections we respect and have expectations about.

There are many novels written from the point of view of a real or imagined sibling; William Faulkner's *The Sound and the Fury* and Pat Conroy's *The Prince of Tides* are two.

TODAY write from the point of view of one of your brothers or sisters, real or imagined. Notice how this shift in point of view changes the language, rhythm, and perspective of your words. Or, write about one of your brothers and sisters, or what you imagine it is like to be your brother or sister.

> The meeting of two personalities is
> like the contact of two chemical
> substances: if there is any reaction,
> both are transformed.
> C . G . J U N G

W H A T ' S   M I S S I N G

WHAT YOU LEAVE OUT of writing must be as deliberate as what you put in. Those brain teasers that ask you to notice what is either missing from or wrong with the picture intensify the way you look at it. So it is with writing.

I don't mean to suggest that you should deliberately omit information as a gimmick to engage the reader. But experimenting with subtracting elements from a descriptive passage helps writers become more nimble at establishing tone and character.

For instance, how would it affect a description of a landscape if you left out all reference to color? Or, how would a dialogue be affected if you eliminated all reference to gender?

Experimental writing is born from such choreography and re-arrangement.

TODAY write or rewrite a piece so that something is left out. Then rewrite it again subtracting a different element. Or, write about something that is missing. You might even make a list of what you miss.

The unsaid, for me, exerts great
power . . .
LOUISE GLÜCK

H I D E - O U T S

SOMETIMES WE WRITE to explore hidden parts of our societies and souls. Other times we use writing as a hide-out or shelter from the same. Both are great reasons to write (and to read). Just as contemplation nourishes us, so does hiatus recharge us. This is one reason many writers work in more than one genre. For instance, if you write poetry that is contemplative and serious you might feel compelled to write humorous essays and prose poems too. It's a kick. And it's a chance to explore in another way.

TODAY write a piece that is a hide-out for you. Or, list ways your characters hide; for instance, shutting the blinds, averting the eyes, or switching off the fax machine. Or, make a list of your personal hide-outs; choose one and describe being there.

> The world I create in writing
> compensates for what the real
> world does not give me.
> GLORIA ANZALDUA

UNFORGETTABLE FOOD

IN A NOVEL like Laura Esquivel's *Like Water For Chocolate* or the biblical narrative of the Last Supper, food is symbolic, metaphorical. Even in daily life, foods are symbols for us.

Pheasant under glass surrounded by wild raspberries is what I imagine chivalry in King Arthur's court tasted like. Champagne and caviar mean wealth and celebration. Spam is a symbol of hardworking, minimum-wage-earning Americans.

Each of us has personal associations with certain foods as well. You get teary remembering grandfather's buckwheat pancakes. You feel disappointed anticipating Aunt Gretchen's dried-out turkey. You can't stand Jell-O after getting it in the hospital every day for two weeks. Food nourishes more than our physical bodies. It feeds our senses, memories, imaginations and souls.

TODAY write about food as a symbol. Your characters may share a meal in which food impacts the action or heightens their relationship. Or, list foods that are symbolic for you. Then, choose one and fill the page with your memories and associations.

Thomas Wolfe ate the world and vomited lava. Dickens dined at a different table every hour of his life. Molière, tasting society, turned to pick up his scalpel . . .
RAY BRADBURY

THE LIVING DEATH

IN WRITING AS IN acting, a death scene can kill the moment more thoroughly than the character if it isn't done well. When writing about death keep the experience alive. Melodrama and cliché will want to pay their condolences; send them packing.

Death is hidden in our culture. Many people have never even seen a corpse. Most of us don't have the experience of witnessing death to draw from.

There are also several aspects to death: funny moments, angry encounters, fear, anxiety, and relief. When writing, it is important to keep in mind that these can be simultaneous experiences for the dying person as well as those who witness the death or discover the body.

Death drives us even when we don't consciously think about it. No matter who we are or what we accomplish, we die; there's no way out. So it is a subject of universal concern and interest.

TODAY write about death. Describe the death you have imagined for yourself. Or, describe a death you witnessed, or someone living whose death you imagine. Write a death scene for one of your characters.

Death is terrifying because it is so ordinary. It happens all the time.
SUSAN CHEEVER

Art is our chief means of breaking bread with the dead.
W. H. AUDEN

S O   L O N G ,   F A R E W E L L ,   A D I E U

SONGWRITER PAUL SIMON says there are fifty ways to leave your lover. There are also at least fifty ways to leave your parents, your children, a dull party, Madison Square Garden, and a state of mind.

Notice the different senses of closure in *so long, farewell,* and *adieu.* *So long* is informal and carefree. *Farewell* holds a wish for the other person to travel on under favorable conditions. *Adieu,* a term we borrow from French, literally means "to God," as if the person saying good-bye leaves the other in God's care.

To leave a person, a place, or a state of mind is to stand at the brink of giving up something familiar for something that is not yet real. It often happens in stages. Exits and partings are the subjects of novels, poems, plays and songs because we are constantly faced with how to leave one stage for the next.

As writers, parting is a fertile study because it is a culminating moment. But an exit is moving only if what leads up to it is convincing. When a character leaves town or a writer moves on to the next paragraph there has to be a reason.

TODAY describe a parting. Write a parting dialogue between two people. Narrate the way you or a character departs from a familiar place; does it include a final tour of the environment or a steady focus on the new destination? Or, make a list of fifty ways to exit a dull conversation.

Every exit is an entry somewhere else.
T O M   S T O P P A R D

PUTTING OUT THE WELCOME MAT

Ships at a great distance have every man's wish on board. For some they come in with the tide. For others they sail forever on the horizon, never out of sight, never landing until the Watcher turns his eyes in resignation, his dreams mocked to death by Time. This is the life of men.

ZORA NEALE HURSTON'S OPENING LINES FROM
THEIR EYES WERE WATCHING GOD

THERE IS A BIG difference between the beginning and the opening of a piece of writing. The first words of a piece are often the last ones the writer wrote. Confusing the opening with the beginning will often keep people from writing. The beginning is what gets you, the writer, to start writing. The opening is what you come up with much later to tempt readers into the experience you've already created for them.

The opening is the doorway in. It may be elegant, menacing, shut tight, or left ajar in order to entice the reader to approach. No matter what tone it takes, the opening serves to get the reader involved.

To arrive at the most effective opening, it is often necessary to write through to the middle or end of the piece to sense what image or information will engage the reader. Opening a story with an elephant charging down a city street chased by a soccer team may get attention, but does it also orient the reader through a combination of tone and information to the world of the piece?

WHAT entices you? How do you like to enter a new environment or get to know someone? Today write about what attracts you and makes you feel welcome; are they the same for you? Or, write eight opening lines that would make you want to read on; now go back to one and write a short synopsis of the piece that would follow it. Notice opening lines in conversations and reading material today.

I D o

WHETHER WE ARE married or single, all of us have strong ideas about marriage. I know of a couple who had a second wedding ceremony six years into their marriage because they felt that they were fulfilling different pledges than they had first made. I also know someone who had a double wedding ceremony in which she married first herself and then her photography. At the reception she told us that now when people quipped that she was married to her job, they would be right.

"I do" are the words that bind us to the pledges we make during a wedding ceremony. Those promises of love, honor, respect, and the commitment to stick around during illness and difficult financial conditions stretch us to our limits and then beyond them.

Each of us is wedded to something or someone in the world. Writers, for instance, are wedded to writing and each of us has a unique marriage.

TODAY write about wedding. Dive in and make a list of associations with the word. Write out the vows you or your character have made to whatever or whomever you are wedded to besides your spouse. Or, create a set of vows for a character or yourself that would end with you committing to the phrase "I do not" rather than "I do."

> I am closer to the work than to anything on earth. That's the marriage.
> LOUISE NEVELSON

B A B Y F A C E

From a child's perspective the world looks different. Giuseppe Tornatore's film *Cinema Paradiso,* Mark Twain's novel *Huck Finn,* Theodore Roethke's poem "My Papa's Waltz" portray the world to us through the eyes and understanding of a child. Actually, though, we are experiencing an adult writer's perception of a child's view.

The adult interpretation of the way a child thinks, experiences, sees, and understands has a lot to do with the way the adult writer remembers childhood, and the order in which the writer crafts the events in the piece. For instance, the entire experience can take place during childhood or as a series of flashbacks.

Also, the writer counts on adult readers to make associations and interpretations of their own.

TODAY write about your childhood or a character's childhood. Or, write from the perspective of a child. Start by describing something simple like getting dressed. You may want to take a few moments to close your eyes and mentally go back to being a child by seeing yourself at a young age or picturing a child you know. When you are finished, experiment with reordering your piece to create room for an adult reader's interpretation. If you wrote about yourself, include one detail that isn't factual but makes sense in the piece.

The poet is the one who is able to keep
the fresh vision of the child alive.
A N A Ï S N I N

YOUR IMAGINATION IS LIKE a kaleidoscope combining and re-combining the elements it contains. The imagination doesn't take orders. But whenever you give it an empty container or a blank page it will fill the space with something.

When we don't interfere with reason, logic or opinions the imaginative mind is mischievous and playful. It's also clever; it makes associations and connections that rationality and contemplation cannot. When you activate this aspect of your imagination you tap into a fascinating source of material.

TODAY create a container and let your imagination play. Do this by taking the phrase, "I used to be . . . but now . . ." and filling in the blanks over and over until you have filled two pages. Work quickly so as not to interfere with the process by having an opinion or wanting what you write to make sense. For example, "I used to egg folks on, but now my enthusiasm is scrambled" and "I used to be a woman, but now I have a child" are two that surfaced from such lists. Decide if any of your phrases make a compelling idea for a short story or a poem.

Rationality squeezes out much that is
rich and juicy and fascinating.
ANNE LAMOTT

PLANTING / GARDENING / HARVESTING

WHEN WE WRITE from experience we harvest our lives. Some of our experiences take a long time to ripen, and not every experience we have is food for other people. Also, not everything we offer is going to be sweet. Some important foods have a bitter taste, like lemon. In writing we must separate what we feed other people from what stays in the field to mulch the next crop.

This is why revision is necessary to creative writing. We have to pick out the details and incidents, cull the food from them. It is not enough to have experiences and record them. This would be like eating the seeds instead of planting them: Something is gained, but it is not created with purpose.

Revising takes the form of adding, cutting, reordering, or changing completely. You must engage in doing what the word *revise* literally means: to see again. This means after working on a piece, you step outside its boundaries and look at it, not through your own eyes but through the eyes of the reader.

This is a difficult stance. It takes practice. It can feel awkward, but unless you go through the process, you end up with a field of wildflowers which may be lovely, but will never be refined.

TODAY take a piece of writing and tend it as a gardener would. Start by seeing it again from the reader's perspective. What is clear? What isn't? Add, cut, reorder. Start to revise.

> Once something is written down, I will
> argue, I will listen to its music, I will
> change, reorder and rewrite.
> SERGE GAVRONSKY

S L I N G I N G   S L A N G

SLANG IS DOUBLE-EDGED language. It can muddy writing. If you describe your character as being *hip* you convey only a superficial sense of his being sophisticated, fashionable, or aware. Using slang can generate imprecise description. It is also distinctly regional as well as dated. *Cool* means dispassionate, pleasing, or in the know depending on which community it's used in. *Groovy* means the opposite of what it meant in the Sixties.

On the other hand, if your character speaks or thinks in slang it can reveal how she perceives her world. If she says her goldfish croaked instead of died it signals the way she views and handles death.

If you always force a character to speak in standard English you risk losing the rhythm, texture, and imagery that emanates from the slang, dialect, or colloquialisms that are natural to him. What if Mark Twain had expunged Huck Finn's Missouri dialect or Louise Erdrich eliminated her characters' Ojibwa expressions?

TODAY write a short description or dialogue using slang. Then rewrite it translating the slang into more conventional phrases. Or, try the same study using a familiar dialect rich in regional expressions. Or, pick a slang expression and write a thirty-two-line poem in which each line repeats the expression and defines the term using a different example. For instance, cool is eating ice cream in the pool/cool is being the last one off the plane and the first one to get a taxi/etc.

Slang is a language that rolls up its
sleeves, spits on its hands and goes
to work.
CARL SANDBURG

ODE TO AN ELBOW

THE RISKIER A SUBJECT is, the more writers rely on form.

These days, praise is riskier to express with dignity than criticism. So writing praise takes practice, practice, practice. First attempts at praise can sound sappy and sentimental, riddled with clichés.

It takes unusual measures to dig deep into this field that is covered in layers of neglected dirt. You have to find a patch with a little give and bounce.

An ode is a song that expresses lofty feelings in a dignified style. It is a form of poetry used for praise and often directly addresses the subject of the poem: O Sun, O Sara, O Destiny.

The body is also neglected by many writers. Several folks I've worked with create disembodied characters who think, converse, and even move from scene to scene without a physical sensation below their necks.

Combining two difficult subjects such as praise and bodies within a form can turn struggle into challenge and fun.

CHOOSE *a part of your body and write an ode to it. Really consider what is praiseworthy about this body part: its function, its appearance, its relationship to the rest of the body. Although there will be a temptation to write for humor, stay with sincerity and see if genuine praise and dignity emerge.*

> Only those that risk going too far can
> possibly find out how far one can go.
> T. S. ELIOT

NEVER SAY NEVER

NEVER IS ONE of the words that writing teachers discourage you from using. It is an overstatement and an oversimplification of the emotions you feel when you are compelled to use it: "I'll never speak to you again!" "I'd never lie to you."

In the first example the *never* expresses anger. In the second it expresses a desire for trust. If a character uses *never* a lot, it becomes a device for revealing a suspect or immature personality. But unless that aspect of the character reappears and plays a role in the unfolding of the narrative the term will seem melodramatic.

There are times when using *never* is both powerful and true to the work, such as in Edgar Allan Poe's "The Raven" when the bird answers ominously "Nevermore" to the narrator's every question. Whenever you are compelled to use *never*, consider what emotion you really want to get across.

OVERSTATEMENT and exaggeration are fun. Purge yourself of the never impulse by using it wildly with abandon all over the page today. In the process, discover what emotions you most often substitute never for. From now on pay close attention when you write from those feelings.

> Avoid words that can't even scratch at
> the hundred hidden meanings in ob-
> jects and structures.
> EDUARDO PAOLOZZI

GOING HOME

WHAT MAKES YOU FEEL at home? Is it a smell, a place, certain music, particular people? In *The Wizard of Oz,* Dorothy chants that there's no place like it. Tracy Kidder has devoted himself and several books to understanding this physical and psychic place called home where we love to be or can't wait to escape.

Home is both a place and a state of mind. It is literal and concrete as well as symbolic and abstract. In all its forms it is a driving force. The great epic poem *The Odyssey* begins with the hero longing for home and the goddess Athena seizing the opportunity to help him while her uncle, the god Poseidon, is away from home.

In its literal form, home is wherever we grew up or now live. It may be a wonderful or a hideous place. Symbolically, home is where we long to be, where we feel we belong. A great deal of drama and narrative is driven by home: getting to, escaping from, defining, and accepting or denying the conflicts inherent in home.

TODAY write about home. Describe your home or a character's home. Or, list attributes of home. Notice what category of details you most often return to: place, people, experience, or something else; whichever category comes up the most is where you feel at home writing. Where else are you at home in your writing?

One writes to make a home for oneself,
on paper, in time, in others' minds.
ALFRED KAZIN

I A L R E A D Y   K N O W

L ET'S GIVE OURSELVES some credit! As writers, we are forever trying to figure out what comes next, or how to improve what is on the page. We forget to enjoy what we have accomplished.

Even if you're at the beginning stages of becoming a writer, there are aspects of the craft you already know. Taking an accounting of what you have will propel you toward another parcel of what you are creating and looking for.

TODAY focus on what you know. You may recount: the plot of your story so far; the relationships between your characters; aspects of the subject you have already explored in a poem. Or, write down everything you can think of that you know about writing; start with constructing a sentence. Or, write the phrase "I already know" as a diving exercise and fill the page with your knowledge.

Do not let great ambitions overshadow
small successes.
FORTUNE COOKIE

WHAT'S NEW

THESE DAYS, *NEW* is associated with *better*. It is a word that is used to persuade people to buy products and ideas. We often find it near *improved*. But like many descriptive words, it has various connotations.

New can mean novel, modern, recent, strange, renovated, recreated, original, fresh, unaccustomed, and the latest. New isn't always better; it is just different. This may at first seem like a small point. It isn't. It is the kind of realization that could be the turning point for your protagonist. To look beyond the surface meaning of a single descriptive word is to find a source of fresh material.

CHOOSE two of the above meanings of new *and explore them in writing either individually or through comparison. Or, write a short piece in which something new is both an improvement and a disadvantage for someone.*

> When I use a word, it means
> what I choose it to mean—neither
> more nor less.
> HUMPTY DUMPTY (LEWIS CARROLL)

JUST BECAUSE

WHAT DO SMALL CHILDREN, writers, first-time parents, and philosophers have in common? They are all devoted to the question WHY: Why is the sky blue? Why are we never satisfied for long? Why won't my baby eat anything but grapes? Why are we here?

Because is the beginning of all answers except *I don't know.* Whenever you write, you are responding to some question inside. A silent *because* starts each piece. But even when you feel a lot of energy and emotion around a piece, it's not always clear what the question is that you're answering.

It's okay to keep writing without knowing why up to a point; often your best material shows up when you keep one eye closed to a question that would overwhelm you into silence if you stared it in the face.

Sometimes you get stranded in the midst of a piece when you can't articulate the question it is answering. When this happens, shift gears and generate a list of answers, each beginning with the word *because,* and the central question may surface.

MAKE a list of twenty-five sentences that begin with because. *Then select one that answers a question you will address in your writing today. Or, read over a piece you are working on that hasn't quite gelled. Now start a new page with the word* because *and fill the page, returning to* because *each time you finish an answer. What questions surface?*

> In art, to admit only what one understands leads to impotence.
> AUGUSTE RODIN

M A C H I N A T I O N S

THE USE OF TOOLS and machines is rare in species other than our own. Most animals come equipped with sufficient anatomical appendages to meet their needs. Our impulse to invent tools is a manifestation of our creative nature as well as a response to necessity.

What if we understood tools and machines as messages from the creative mind about aspects of our nature? For instance, consider a paper clip: a small, pliable, portable device for keeping ideas together. As humans, we fasten ideas and perceptions together in ways that are firm but can be easily changed.

TODAY choose any tool or machine and, in detail, first describe it physically, then describe its uses. Next, through writing, consider how the device corresponds to an aspect of human nature. Start with the phrase "Consider the _____" and fill in the blank with the device of your choice. Pay attention to the tools and machines you use today.

All the tools and engines on earth
are only extensions of man's
limbs and senses.
RALPH WALDO EMERSON

O R I G I N S

WHERE WE COME FROM influences both what we write and how we write. But our origins are not only geographical and cultural. We originate from all of the sources that have directed and shaped our lives. They include books, movies, neighborhoods, landscapes, sayings, people, foods, clothing, anything and everything that has left a deep impression on our way of seeing the world.

This is why six people can describe the same tree differently. Each person sees it through a unique set of experiences. One recognizes the genus, another imagines it as a figure with arms outstretched, a third spots the quickest route to the top. Cliché seeps into writing when writers forget or neglect to bring who they are into the piece.

"Origin" comes from the Latin *orior:* I rise, become visible. Your subject and style rises and becomes visible when you reveal yourself.

TODAY write about your origins. Start with the phrase, "I come from." Include words and sounds you remember hearing, smells, tastes, and sites. Write about all those things which, had you not known them, would have significantly altered who you are.

Experience is not what happens to
you; it is what you do with
what happens to you.
ALDOUS HUXLEY

I F O N L Y

HOW MANY TIMES a person starts a thought with this conditional phrase! "*If only* I had purchased that stock when I had the chance," and she is off and running with visions of the ways life would be different. Or, "*If only* I hadn't lied in the first place," and he sees himself exonerated. Having expectations and hopes are acts of the imagination. Sure, for many people, "if only" is a cry of regret. But for writers it can be the source of the next piece; it is the imagination at work again.

TODAY make a list of "if onlys"—yours or your character's. Fill one page. There may be one that suggests the next section in the piece you are writing, or an idea for a new piece. Or, see if linking a few "if onlys" from the list generates something new.

> We write to taste life twice, in the moment, and in retrospection.
> ANAÏS NIN

I, You, He, She, It, We, They

THE TITLE OF THIS study is a grammar review. If grammar makes you cringe, join the club. I was schooled in the Seventies during an innovative, well-meaning era of curriculum reform that included a new approach to teaching English in which we didn't learn terms such as "pronoun," "adjective," and "verb."

To this day I struggle with grammatical terms and concepts; the thought of diagramming a sentence causes me to break out in hives. But I am a writer; despite my discomfort, I am responsible for mastering this all-important tool of my art. I don't use my inadequacy as an excuse for not writing, or not imbibing, a bit at a time, what doesn't come easily to me.

Now for the fun part. Pronouns are also a list of choices you have when you decide which point of view to write from. First-, second-, and third-person narratives place both the reader and the writer in differing proximity to the narrator and other characters.

When you're stuck in the midst of a piece, change the point of view, for example, from first person to third to gain perspective; creating the extra distance often allows you more objectivity.

TODAY take a piece of your writing and switch the point of view. If you were writing in third person (he/she, they, it), rewrite in first person, or try second (you) and see what develops. Or, use pronouns to generate material; list the pronouns down the page and let each one start a line or a paragraph: I am the woman eating a grape/you are watching me/he . . . , and so on.

The writer's point of view is a choice
among tools.
TRACY KIDDER

B O R D E R   T O W N

WRITING IS A border town between experience, imagination, and understanding. Borders are wild and unstable places so it's a good idea to be as centered as possible when visiting them. The reason writers often surround their writing time with rituals such as jumping rope, making coffee, or rearranging piles of paper is that these are ways to prepare for the trip.

You enter another time zone. You go alone. Every time. Cyberspace and the information highway are not nearly as amazing or as interesting. Writers pitch a tent between three states of mind and start to explore.

Borders are a big subject in writing because living means constantly crossing them between the physical, emotional, spiritual, and psychological realms. This is where two or more places meet, where one ends, another begins, but both exist at the same time. One reason politically imposed geographical borders create conflict is they don't take into account emotional, psychological, and spiritual borders which can't always be distinguished in physical space.

TODAY write about borders. Use what you know from personal encounters about moving between experience and understanding. Or, consider what you know about your own writing process and how you move from idea to idea as you write, how the words, the images, the sounds come to you.

I know I walk in and out of several
worlds every day.
JOY HARJO

Turn on the Light

In Western literature, light is a symbol of truth, clarity, awakening, knowledge, or a turn for the better. But not everyone loves the light. In Tennessee Williams's "A Streetcar Named Desire," Blanche DuBois avoids light, along with the truth of her aging and circumstances.

In our day to day existence different types of light affect us in distinct ways; we use lighting to create atmosphere and mood: fluorescent light for work, dim light for romance, spotlights for attention. We use light the same way in the written world. But if you automatically use sunlight to portray awakening when in reality sunlight hurts your eyes, the writing will be clichéd instead of moving. Even when using time-honored symbols, you must stay true to your own experience.

Today consider, in writing, the types of light that affect you most, and how. When you work with light in a piece of writing remember to turn on the bright truth of your own leanings.

Artists and poets must find the light in
which they can find themselves.
Frances Kelly

G L O W   I N   T H E   D A R K

D ARKNESS, IN WESTERN LITERATURE, is associated with mystery, danger, sensuality, what is hidden, curved, female, and lost. The state of darkness for a character or a place can include any combination of emotion, spirit, and psyche. In writing, it often manifests physically.

For instance, a writer might introduce a town about to undergo a moral crisis during an overcast day rather than a sunny one, or the woman in the midst of a spiritual journey sitting at a café table shadowed by an adjacent temple.

The challenge is to use darkness effectively without being heavy-handed. Try to remain grounded in the concrete details of the description and not mention the darkness merely as a symbol.

In the case of the woman at the café, describing the temple's shadow might also explain why her friend had trouble spotting her. So the shadow is a functional as well as symbolic element of the scene. Symbols are suspect if they exist only for their own sake.

TODAY write your character into a state or place of darkness that isn't gratuitous. Or, list your personal associations with darkness.

In the dark time, the eye begins to see.
T H E O D O R E   R O E T H K E

SIGNS OF AGE

EVERYTHING AND EVERYONE ages. It is an unavoidable experience. Consider the ways we view the aging process. When wine ages, it becomes more valued and coveted. When a woman ages she is encouraged to do everything she can to make it appear it isn't happening; otherwise it is implied she will lose her value. In thinking about the older women you know, is it true that they have less to offer than younger ones?

Observation is one of a writer's most valuable tools. If you become lax in your use of it your writing suffers; you begin to rely on stereotype, cliché, and the insistent imagery of trends.

TODAY observe a tree, a house, a book, or yourself and describe signs of aging. Remember to use touch, sound, and smell. When you have finished, read over your description; if it depicts only decay or reverence, return to your subject and broaden your observations.

After a certain number of years, our
faces become our biographies.
CYNTHIA OZICK

THE ANTI-YOU

IN LITERATURE AND DRAMA an antihero is a main character who is not heroic in the sense of having an especially moral character or providing exceptional service to humanity. Not all antiheroes are evil. Charlotte Brontë's Jane Eyre is a hero. Anne Rice's vampire Lestat is an antihero. But Flaubert's Madame Bovary and Anne Tyler's Maggie Moran in *Breathing Lessons* are antiheroes. Gene Roddenberry's "Star Trek" captains Kirk and Picard are heroes; Woody Allen's protagonists are antiheroes. You get the idea.

Just as antiheroes are provocative characters, so is the anti-you. Think about the anti-you as being your shadow writer. This is the underbelly of your urge to write. Remember, the anti-you or shadow writer isn't necessarily evil. It is the part of you that turns up your nose at romance writing or science fiction, the part that can't understand the big fuss about detective stories or horror. If you have a strong feeling about a genre, even a negative feeling, there is energy surrounding it to tap into and use.

TODAY pick a style or genre that you haven't worked in before, especially one you feel negative toward: romance, allegory, realism, sci-fi, or any other. Use yourself as the main character or narrator and depict something you have trouble writing about, such as sex, childhood, or landscape. You can try the same scene in as many venues as you like. Now return to your own style and notice if you've gained some ground.

It is never too late to be who you might
have been.
GEORGE ELIOT

O P P O S I T E S   A T T R A C T

ONE WAY TO DEVELOP a narrative is to create a character and listen to her story. We each create characters differently. Some writers base their characters on aspects of themselves; others base characters on people the writer notices in public places (who are also aspects of the writer); yet others base characters on family, friends, and acquaintances.

The difficulty in creating a character from someone you know is that most of your opinions are already formed. This doesn't serve you when the impulse is to describe your character flirting with the bartender when you know that in real life she is too shy to flirt. Reality can get in your way.

But your friends have lives that interest you, so you may want to write about them. One way to use friends in creating characters is to first write sketches of their opposites and then develop a character based on how your friend might react to his opposite. Another way is to make a character ten years younger or older than its real-life counterpart.

TODAY create a character based on a friend of yours by either changing his age or developing her opposite. After a page or two of description have your character speak to you or vice versa. Or, make a list of all your friends and group them by their characteristics. Notice which traits keep surfacing and create one character with these traits and one with opposite traits.

To know one thing, you must know the opposite.
H E N R Y   M O O R E

I tell my students you have an absolute right to write about people you know and love. You *do*. But the kicker is you have a responsibility to make the characters large enough that you will not have sinned against them.
D O R O T H Y   A L L I S O N

O L D

A SINGLE WORD can have many meanings just as a color has many shades. As writers, we explore the shadings of a word as a painter explores a color. We can also look to a word's etymology to understand it better. A thesaurus is an excellent tool for this research, as is *The Oxford English Dictionary.*

Take the word *old.* It can mean worn out, weakened, ancient, famous, long-standing, familiar, venerable, antique, antiquated, archaic, obsolete, former, or grand. Its meaning shouldn't be left to the reader's associations; it is the writer's job to set the meaning or multiple meanings through the tone and context of the word, so it is clear when Segewick consults the "old" book whether it is obsolete or venerable.

PICK four of the above meanings of old. *Make sure at least two of your choices are ones you don't often consider. Beneath each choice list at least fifteen things that you would describe as reflecting that quality.*

> To select well among old things is almost equal to inventing new ones.
> NICOLAS CHARLES TRUBLET

I STILL DON'T KNOW

ONE OF THE BIG secrets of writing is that you learn by *doing*. Writing is a process of discovery. Some folks who attend workshops and classes arrive expecting me to tell them how to write. They feel disappointed when, instead, I suggest ideas to write about and ways to craft and revise what they've already written.

If you are stuck at page eighty-seven in your novel, I can't tell you what to write next; nobody can. Because it is your novel, not mine, all I can do is send you back into it suggesting a window or door that may dead-end or lead to the rest of the house.

Even if someone could tell you what to write next or how to fix what you've already written, it would rob you of your purpose. The impulse to *learn* is the fundamental force that drives us to write. The most anyone can do is to tell you what they understand in your work, what they wonder about when reading it, how it makes them feel, and what literary devices might be helpful. The rest is up to you.

TODAY celebrate what you still don't know. Make a list of the elements you are unsure of in the plot of your story; the ideas as yet undeveloped in a poem; or the point of an essay that hasn't yet crystallized. These are your reasons to keep on writing. Or, write the phrase "I still don't know" as a diving study and fill the page with whatever comes out. Select one thing you don't know to write/learn about today.

Experience is a hard teacher. She gives
the test first, the lesson afterward.
ANONYMOUS

DANGER ZONES

> The images we invent could change
> into wild beasts and tear us to pieces.
> RUMI

RUMI IS RIGHT. Take the vision of nuclear weapons and the concept of a master race as examples. The imaginative mind is as capable of creating evil as it is good. Willing ourselves not to imagine what we believe is dangerous won't work. A fundamental element of imagination is that it cannot be controlled for long. Censorship grows out of a belief that it can be. This is one reason why censorship eventually fails.

What you can control is what you do with your dangerous imaginings. If you ignore or deny them, they grow into beasts and rip away at you. When folks tell me that they write because they'd go crazy if they didn't, I think this is what they mean. Writing serves to contain the images.

If you avoid what is dangerous, you avoid life. If you throw yourself into a dangerous place without preparation, you devalue life. Writing is one of the crossroads where what is most disturbing can be explored and investigated without destroying yourself or others. This is one of the highest purposes of the arts.

As writers we have a responsibility to name our danger zones, prepare ourselves and bring them to the empty page in as small or as large portions as are manageable.

TODAY move into the danger zone. You may want to prepare yourself with some deep breathing or other centering activity. Go as far as you can into your dangerous images: list some of the most horrible, hideous thoughts you ever had, or describe one in detail. When you are finished draw a box or circle around the words to contain them. If you must, tear up the page or erase the file.

F R U I T S   O F   T H E
F O R B I D D E N
(E A T I N G   T H E   A P P L E)

INDULGING IN WHAT IS forbidden is delicious. The temptation creates passion, the anticipation is thrilling: the heart races, breath quickens, the mind becomes one-pointed, the senses attuned like a wild animal hunting prey—anxiety mounts at the thought of being found out, guilt and the giddiness of freedom pump through your temples. These are the fruits of the forbidden.

The forbidden is not exactly the same as the dangerous. Often the forbidden is perceived as dangerous, but the essence of forbidden is that an authority is imposing a prohibition on the act. The power relationship this sets up stokes our desire to challenge authority and risk the behavior on several levels: personal, familial, and societal. This is one of the oldest stories written and told. It is the story of Eve and the Apple, Prometheus stealing fire from the gods, Frankenstein.

When something is forbidden it becomes more desirable. As a teenager, I was forbidden to ride on motorcycles. I'll always savor the first time I put on a helmet, swung my leg over the back seat, grabbed the denim-bound, bony hips of a college sophomore, and whipped down the FDR Drive.

EXPLORE the forbidden today. Begin with a memory, something already risked. Recapture, in writing, the sensual experience; make up what you don't recall. Or, approach something currently forbidden: an affair, belching in public, eating a whole chocolate cake by yourself. Risk it on paper; it's authentic when you feel the physical thrill.

Your soul grows sick with longing for
the things it has forbidden itself.
OSCAR WILDE

Y OU ARE A good place to begin when creating a character. You've known yourself longer than you've known anyone else. But how do you move beyond that five-foot-six, dark-haired, nearsighted adventurer? One answer lies in focusing on and exaggerating various aspects of yourself through different characters.

If you're anything like me, you can list attributes about yourself and there will be more negative ones than positive ones. This list is the character you believe you are. But it's just one version of yourself. When you act "out of character" it is only another aspect of yourself emerging. Who is that? How would that part of you respond to shocking news, or the car breaking down?

TODAY develop a character sketch of an alter ego: organized where you are disorganized, short if you are tall, and so on. Remember that this character isn't a better version of you, but another version of what you love and don't love about yourself. When you are finished, notice how you feel about this character; what aspects intrigue you? How does the character fit into the subjects and themes you are currently writing about? Give this character a name.

There are so many selves in
everybody and to explore and
exploit just one is wrong, dead wrong,
for the creative person.
J A M E S   D I C K E Y

THE FUNNIEST THINGS

YOU *CAN* WRITE humor. Funny things happen all the time. We trade these humorous anecdotes with our family and friends. In the telling, we shape stories, narrate events.

One aspect of the story is the event itself. But the funniest storytellers also use facial expressions, tone of voice and body language to emphasize the personality of the characters involved.

Another element is timing. Good storytellers don't always relate events chronologically, and they pause during descriptions and explanations for emphasis or to create suspense. Humor relies on this type of crafting.

TODAY write down, verbatim, a funny anecdote that you've heard or told many times, one that always makes you chuckle. Go back into the narration and craft it for the written world focusing on timing and the order of events. Later you can return to the story and develop the characters.

> My mother wanted us to understand
> that the tragedies of your life one day
> have the potential to be the comic
> stories the next.
> NORA EPHRON

T R U E   C O N F E S S I O N S

I AM VISITING the Pacific Northwest in the dead of winter and it isn't rainy and overcast for the first time in a week. I am writing as I do most days at this time.

I want to go outside and take a walk in the woods before it gets dark or clouds up again. If I go now instead of in two hours, I will have to first shower and change out of my pajamas. To do this I will have to leave the living room and pass by a shelf with five books I really want to read, the mail, and the dirty dishes in the sink. I wanted to start writing a couple of hours earlier, but my partner who I'm here with had a rough night; it was my turn to be the support.

I came out here so I would have fewer distractions and could concentrate on this book. And I do have fewer distractions here than at home. But I am a writer; I am easily distracted—the two often go together. My interest, curiosity, desire for order, empathy are part of what call me to write at the same time as they call me away from the page.

So I will stay at the desk and keep the distractions at bay a bit longer. I can glance out the window and take in this clear, sunny day between pages . . . but not for too long.

TODAY, as you write, incorporate into the piece some of what you would like to be doing right now if you weren't writing.

. . . Think of all the other writers out there in the world, taking the same detour from word processor to coffeepot, thesaurus in hand, hopes in tow. We're all in it together, crossing over and over the elusive bridge between words and literature.
A B B Y   F R U C H T

We're all in this together—by ourselves.
L I L Y   T O M L I N

M Y   C A R ,   M Y   S E L F

A WOMAN I MET in Los Angeles once said to me, "Honey, 'round here you are your car!" Since I didn't own a car at the time, I felt like a nobody, although the same woman assured me that having no car was definitely better than riding around L.A. in a boring one.

The way people drive reveals even more about their personalities than what they drive. But I liked the idea of being a car. From childhood, I remember a TV comedy called "My Mother the Car." When the woman reincarnated as a car got angry with her son she'd whack him on the backside with her door.

I know someone who can name the make and year of every American car built between 1952 and 1968 on sight from two blocks away. Don't you know someone like that? Cars are meaningful in America.

TODAY pick someone you know and describe that person driving a car. Or, describe a car, its look and the way it drives as if it were a friend of yours. Or, describe your first car, or the first time you were in the driver's seat. Or, name every make and model car you can think of and what meaning each has for you.

> No manmade device since the shields
> and lances of knights quite fulfills a
> man's ego like an automobile.
> W I L L I A M   R O O T E S

A
C R O S T I C

An ACROSTIC IS the poetry exercise you were assigned in fifth grade. If your teacher skipped that part of the curriculum, let me catch you up. An acrostic is when the first letter of each line of a poem spells out a word or phrase that is usually the subject of the poem. Most of us first learned to write acrostic poems using our names.

Acrostics are helpful openings for material you have difficulty penetrating. Write the topic in a word or phrase vertically down the page, giving each letter its own line. Then set to work creating one statement or image that begins with each letter of the phrase. An important aspect of using this method is to create written lines of more than two or three words. You don't have to attempt to connect one line to the next, although clusters of related material may develop. You may not use the material you create this way in the actual piece, but you almost always find one or more of the lines work as a springboard for developing the piece further.

TODAY use this acrostic study to generate material. Choose a subject and create an acrostic poem. Note—sometimes in this type of poem the vertical word or phrase delivers a sort of counterpoint message to the horizontal poem rather than reflecting the subject. You can construct your acrostic this way, too.

> What I like to do is treat words as a craftsman does
> his wood or stone or what-have-you, to hew,
> carve, mould, coil, polish, and plane them into
> patterns, sequences, sculptures, figures of sound
> expressing some lyrical impulse, some spiritual
> doubt or conviction, some dimly realized truth
> that I must try to reach and realize.
> DYLAN THOMAS

A N O T H E R   P L A N E T

O NE OF MY STUDENTS brought in a story in which the main character was raped in a boathouse and left to make her way back to the road. She was picked up by a driver who turned out to be a rape crisis counselor.

All of us in the class agreed that it was too coincidental to have the driver be a rape crisis counselor. "But that's really how it happened," explained the writer. "Yes," I said, "and thank God it did, but it detracts from the credibility of the story." Although it is often based on a real experience, a narrative is constructed, manipulated, and intentional, whereas life is mysterious and unpredictable.

Of course, as a writer you want to expose, celebrate, and rail against the unpredictable nature of life, but to do so you mustn't confuse fact with truth. Fact is what actually happened: the events as they occurred. In creative writing, truth is anything that evokes, for the reader, the emotional or revelatory experience that inspired the writer.

But writing is another planet with its own natural laws. If you've ever stood on those scales in planetariums that calculate what your weight would be on Saturn or Mars, it isn't equal to your weight on Earth because the rules of gravity are different. So it is with writing; time, weight, everything is different.

BRIEFLY describe a significant event that really happened. Identify the truth you gleaned from the experience. Then create a different, fictional event that reveals the same truth. Don't despair if it seems contrived: it takes a lot of practice; you're now one step closer to getting it.

. . . Facts can obscure the truth.
M AYA A NGELOU

No Experience Necessary

My FIRST COLLEGE writing teacher told me to stick to personal experiences. I wrote about climbing into the washing machines of kind-looking men at the laundromat, and eating lo mein with heroin users while watching football with the sound turned down and the Allman Brothers cranked up. Back then it was hard for my teacher to imagine that I was writing from my experience of feeling desperately lonely and wanting to escape, of innocence poking around in deviancy and finding football. I wanted a good grade. For the final assignment I made up a story about a young girl who anticipates going off to college. I got an A; my teacher felt successful.

"Write about what you know!"—the cry of the writing teacher (mentioned at least as often as "show, don't tell"). It's good advice; I've said it myself. But know where: in your heart, your imagination, your physical life? There are several ways to know anything: experience, research, observation, empathy, association. You have to practice all your ways of knowing.

TODAY write about something you haven't done: piloting an airplane, skinning an animal, teaching English as a second language, water-skiing. It could be something you've read about or observed. Feel free to make up names for unfamiliar pieces of equipment, theories, or methods. Use concrete, specific details. Don't be concerned with accuracy or believability. Instead follow your feelings and your imagination.

The really great writers are people like
Emily Brontë who sit in a room and
write out of their limited experience
and unlimited imagination.
JAMES A. MICHENER

S O U N D   B I T E

Even if you don't speak it aloud, the sound of a word evokes tone and texture beyond its definition. Listen to the difference between "slice" and "cut," "baffling" and "difficult." In both word pairs the first synonym is fluid and the second is harsh. Reading for sound and rewriting for it helps to tune your writing.

When folks ask for guidance reworking a draft I often ask them to listen while I read it aloud to hear whether the sounds conflict or are consistent with the mood of their topic. Tune in to the words I picked to write this study.

TODAY write a paragraph or a short poem about anything that is harsh or hard. Now go back into the piece and replace as many words as you can with harder-sounding synonyms. Use a thesaurus.

> This is the feeling for syllable and
> rhythm, penetrating far below the
> conscious levels of thought and feeling,
> invigorating every word.
> T. S. Eliot

D ID YOU CLEAN the bathroom?"

"Yeah."

"You call that clean?"

This is a familiar exchange. It develops out of two different definitions of the same word. To some, a clean bathroom means scrubbed down with disinfectant. To others it means the trash can isn't spilling over. And "clean" isn't the only concept with multiple definitions. A classic setup for a romance novel is for two people to discover they have different definitions of love's meaning and obligations.

As a writer it is your job to define the terms you or your characters use by revealing the definitions of abstract words like "clean," "love," and "beauty" through action, exchanges between characters, metaphors, and tone or attitude in the narrator's voice.

ANSWER the question "When is it clean?" You can set up a dialogue; describe in detail when a room is sufficiently clean; comment on somebody else's idea of clean; use metaphor to explain it, or even define what is clean by describing what doesn't pass the cleanliness test in your book. Indulge in great amounts of detail. Let your imagination wash over every surface, corner and cranny of the bathroom, refrigerator, or closet.

After ecstasy, the laundry.
ZEN SAYING

GENDER STUDIES

Is it a boy or a girl?" It's the first question we ask when a child is born. The answer refers to more than anatomical equipment, it establishes a reference point for treating a child as masculine or feminine. When a girl is called a tomboy or a boy is described as sensitive it is because they are treading at the borders of our concepts of femininity and masculinity.

Many writers have explored these borders. The title character of Virginia Woolf's *Orlando* incarnates in various centuries as different sexes. In Greek mythology Tiresias lives both as a man and a woman. Jeanette Winterson crafted her novel *Written on the Body* so the narrator's sex is not identified.

How do you create characters of both sexes and all the points in between? Experiment.

TODAY experiment with identity or biology in writing. Use a character you've created or a real-life person. Change their sex or bring them to one edge or the other of the sex they are. As you write, notice how you construct gender. What you notice will help you to create characters that aren't the same sex as you.

Male and female represent the two sides
of the great radical dualism. But, in
fact, they are perpetually passing into
one another.
MARGARET FULLER

A GAIN & A GAIN & A GAIN

"I HEARD YOU the first time!" But what did you hear?

We repeat ourselves when we don't think we've been heard, for emphasis, when we want something remembered, when we are longing. Children love to hear the same story over and over again.

The first time you hear a phrase or sentence you listen for the meaning: pass the peas; I love you; I think, therefore I am. The second, fourteenth, and hundredth times, you experience deeper responses as if the phrase had become a bell whose sound waves resonate throughout you.

Repetition has negative capabilities as well. Nagging or a repetitive task can dull your attention. The old punishment for misbehaving in class was copying "I will not speak out until called on" one hundred times on the chalkboard after school. At either end of the spectrum, repetition moves you into an altered or heightened state by containing your energy inside of or away from the repetition; it is a kind of meditation.

As a study, it is an excellent device for getting to the bones of our imagination and ideas. The rhythm pacifies the internal censor which allows deeper responses to surface.

TODAY choose a phrase and write it down fifty times. Don't shortchange your-self by doing fewer than fifty. Each time, respond to the phrase in one or two sentences or phrases before the next repetition. Work quickly without stopping to think. Anything goes. When you're finished, notice which responses feel surprising, dangerous, charged. What poems, stories, or songs can begin from these strands?

For constructing any work of art you need some
principle of repetition or recurrence.
NORTHROP FRYE

S U P E R S T I T I O U S

S TEP ON A CRACK and break your mother's back.

The dictionary defines superstition as a belief that is inconsistent with known facts, even though the word itself comes from the Latin *superstitio*—a standing in awe of.

Superstitions and old wives' tales, like myths, are rooted in belief systems that recognize magic and imagination as real, necessary, and fundamental forces. If you hold your breath while passing a cemetery, throw salt over your shoulder, and avoid walking under ladders, it isn't simply out of habit but to honor the power you harness to create.

It is helpful to inventory the superstitions you know by committing them to writing. They may reappear as attributes of your characters, as foreshadowing in a plot; they may enter your poems, unearth an image, or suggest a direction for a current piece you're working on.

TODAY write down all the superstitions and old wives' tales you know. Choose one. Describe how you came to learn it. Describe who you first remember teaching it to you.

The world is made up of stories, not
of atoms.
M U R I E L   R U K E Y S E R

D O W N   U N D E R

THINK ABOUT THE ROOMS in your home. Some rooms lend themselves readily to corresponding metaphors in the psyche; take the basement, for instance. It is a storage space that holds what we aren't using right now but might need later. Basements range from well-lit, organized, and immaculate to dark, musty, and cluttered. Sometimes its state is in keeping with the person's style of living and other times it is the opposite.

Basements are hidden places; they're full of what we won't get rid of, but don't use.

TODAY describe your basement and probe its contents in writing. Pay attention to all your senses. Notice whether what you discover has symbolic potential.

A discovery is said to be an accident
meeting a prepared mind.
ALBERT SZENT-GYORGYI

EVERYTHING'S GOING RIGHT

WRITERS PRACTICE FANTASY for its own sake. Fantasy is the playground, the laboratory, the test site. If you fear heights and fantasize about parachuting, you won't get hurt and can still experience a physical exhilaration.

Most people aren't practiced in imagining the best possible scenario without being cautious about it. Some folks use affirmations to balance their negative thoughts. Others have learned through great disappointment not to get their hopes up too high. Those who follow the "hope for the best and expect the worst" philosophy often spend more time preparing for the worst than imagining the best.

BEGIN at the beginning of this day and describe in vivid detail how it would progress if everything went right. Fantasize on paper. Now look over what you've written and, without judging yourself, first enjoy the buzz and then notice if the emphasis is on the material, social, emotional, spiritual, public, or private aspects of your day. How does your perfect day relate to the values and visions of the heroes in your writing?

> We have been taught to believe that
> negative equals realistic and positive
> equals unrealistic.
> SUSAN JEFFERS

H A I R S T O R Y

ALMOST EVERY CULTURE has myths and stories surrounding hair as a symbol of power, beauty or strength. When I ask folks to write about hair, pens fly. Everyone has a hair story and it is usually funny or touching.

Hair is our fur. It is our coat. We attend to it lavishly. Its length, color, texture, and shape can identify us ethnically, socially, and familially. Most of us have visceral memories of rituals associated with hair, like shaving or going to the beauty parlor. One of my favorite pleasures is being shampooed. My haircutter massages my head and bathes my scalp in streams of warm water that run through my hair. Touch your hair now. Did you feel the hair on your head, your arm, your face, your armpit? Wherever you touched are strands of stories, images, and associations.

TODAY write down a hairstory. Or, list images and associations that occur to you when you think about hair.

Rastafarians regard their dreadlocks as
"high tension cables to heaven."
DIANE ACKERMAN

A N A T O M Y   O F   A   T R E E

IN MYTHOLOGY, FOLKTALES, and some belief systems, the vegetal world has another life, a parallel life. Remember the apple tree in *The Wizard of Oz* who scolds Dorothy for picking his fruit? Some would say the apple tree was being given human abilities but this interpretation doesn't acknowledge the consciousness that already exists within the tree. Once you perceive an object as a conscious entity, your imagination recognizes its will. You connect to another level of knowing. Trust it.

TODAY describe the anatomy of a tree: roots, bark, sap, trunk, branches, leaves. Instead of accepting a conventional relationship to trees, see the tree as something, anything, else: a country, a church, earth's hair, a lover. . . .

> I like trees because they seem more re-
> signed to the way they have to live than
> other things do.
> WILLA CATHER

WALLACE STEVENS'S PINEAPPLE

WHAT IF YOU HAD never seen a pencil before? How would you attempt to comprehend it if there were no one to explain it to you?

Writing about ordinary, familiar objects this way refreshes them. Children are good at this because they haven't been locked in by convention. Writers must develop the capacity to see as if it were new something they've seen a million times. The poet Wallace Stevens was brilliant at this. In one poem he describes a pineapple as yesterday's volcano, an owl with a hundred eyes, the sea spraying from rock. Stevens learned to look past what we recognize as a pineapple. He opened his mind to creative vision: the seeing of things in relation to each other through comparison, association, and metaphor.

Every now and then this vision sends a beacon. You turn your head and see the piano keys as a row of teeth or cemetery plots. But more often you stare at objects for a long time before the mind loosens its grip on connecting objects to name to function and creative vision takes over.

TODAY pick an ordinary object and pretend you've never seen it before. Or stare at it until creative vision takes over. It may take a long time or start transforming right away. List all the things it looks like or reminds you of, however remotely. List at least fifteen. Don't choose a photograph, poster, or picture.

The poem refreshes the world.
WALLACE STEVENS

S C A T   W R I T I N G

*A*ND THE MOON ROSE *over the ocean.* Say it aloud. What kind of moon (crescent, full, half) has risen? All the O sounds and letters connect us to the image of a full moon. Besides helping to establish tone and mood, the sounds of words can, almost imperceptibly, add to their meaning.

R, J, M, and N are some of the softer sounds in our alphabet. K, D, and Q are some of the hard sounds. There are also letters and combinations of letters that create full, thin, or open sounds. These are the notes that produce the music. The music of words accompanies their meanings.

Musicians play scales, painters make quick sketches, ballet dancers execute pliés and tondues to warm up before delving into their arts. They do this in order to connect and infuse their tools with their souls so their whole beings pulse with the methods they use to express the spirit within. As writers we must also work to absorb our tools so that they become second nature. Sound is one of these tools.

*T*ODAY *write for music instead of meaning. It may not make sense, grammatically; just place words together for their sound relationships. You can write a soft, full, staccato, or open piece, or you might work on something in which the music changes; notice which types of language come most naturally to you and which demand a greater effort.*

For me, writing is a question of finding
a certain rhythm. I compare it to the
rhythm of jazz.
F R A N Ç O I S E   S A G A N

S I L E N C E

WHAT IF YOU HAVE absolutely nothing to say? Here you have this mind in constant motion and you get ready to write and your mind is a blank. Zippo. Nothing.

You have arrived at a powerful province of your imagination. Write about it.

How do you express silence in writing? This is a tricky feat. All kinds of artists eventually must confront the realm of silence within their mediums. The choreographer Paul Taylor was scheduled to dance his newest work. On opening night Mr. Taylor came out on stage and stood completely still for the duration of the piece. One critic responded with columns of blank space where the review was to appear.

Silence in writing also exists in the space around the words and between the lines. It slips between images, thoughts; it is always there. When you are confronted with a long moment of silence, breathe deeply, close your eyes, enter it.

TODAY explore silence. This may take the form of describing the absence of sound, writing down memories and images you associate with silence, or reworking a piece of writing on the page, being mindful of the silences between words, lines, and sections.

As before, there is a great silence,
with no end in sight. The writer
surrenders, listening.
JAYNE ANNE PHILLIPS

B R E A S T S

I REMEMBER BEING ELEVEN years old and going to the sauna with my mother at the local Y. There were always several naked women of various ages lounging on the benches talking. Each woman's breasts were a unique combination of color, size, shape, texture, nipples. My breasts were just beginning to develop and I glanced at these women in wonder. Galway Kinnell's "My Mother's R & R" is a stirring poem in which two young brothers revisit their infancy at their mother's breasts.

Whether you are a man or a woman, your first awakening to breasts is usually a memorable one. Breasts are deeply symbolic in most cultures. They embody sensuality and nurturance in a single form. Breasts evoke strong emotions ranging from humor to anguish.

For some folks this is an uncomfortable topic. All the more reason to approach it. While there are some subjects you will approach cautiously, avoiding writing about what makes you uncomfortable is a type of self-censorship which is not conducive to broadening your imaginative terrain. So when a difficult topic appears, enter it any way you can, but enter it.

TODAY *write about breasts. You may free associate, recall one or more memories, describe a fantasy. You could even be a breast.*

You long to see how much pleasure I
will let flow through my nipples like
milk . . . perhaps in your mouth,
perhaps on my own hands for
me to lick off.
M I N N I E   B R U C E   P R A T T

122

B I T I N G   T H E   B U L L E T

> You can be a little ungrammatical if
> you come from the right part of
> the country.
> R O B E R T   F R O S T

T HE IMAGINATION OF a language is revealed in its idioms. Rich in imagery, distinctly regional, they appear in all languages. Because idiomatic phrases don't mean what they literally say, their interpretation relies on the collective understanding of a people.

Idioms can be metaphoric like hitting the nail on the head, or metaphysical like you're out of your mind. And many idioms have historical roots. "Bite the bullet" is an idiomatic phrase peculiar to American English that means to confront a painful situation bravely. But it originates from a patient biting a bullet to avoid crying out during battlefield surgery without anesthetic.

It is said that you're truly fluent in a language when you can speak it idiomatically. How fluent are you in your own tongue?

TODAY write down an idiomatic phrase you or someone you know uses often, and dive for half of a page. Then change one word in the phrase, write down the new version, and dive for another half of a page. Or, list as many idioms as you can think of and flag your favorite ones. Take a moment to visualize the literal translations of your favorites. For instance, envision yourself actually biting a bullet; taste the metal in your mouth. For the rest of the day, jot down others that occur to you or that you overhear and add them to your list.

THE MUSIC IN YOU

WHAT IS YOUR INSTRUMENT? Not necessarily the one you took lessons in as a child, but the one you are. Concentrate on musical instruments. See yourself in your mind's eye. Feel what it is like to live in your body. Hear your voice. Examine your hands. Read over your latest piece of writing. What instrument do you experience?

You develop a writing voice just as a musician develops an affinity with an instrument. In a metaphoric way the writer's voice corresponds to a musical instrument. Take a moment to consider a couple of your favorite authors; what musical instruments are they? Now consider yourself.

TODAY write about what instrument you are. Be sure to touch on several of the aspects mentioned above. Or, to explore range, work on a poem or short piece in which you write like an instrument that is unlike you.

> Music is your own experience, your
> thoughts, your wisdom. If you don't
> live it, it won't come out your horn.
> CHARLIE PARKER

B A T H R O O M S   Y O U ' V E
K N O W N

W HAT ABOUT SETTINGS you take for granted because you consider them only functional: subway cars, elevators, bathrooms? Think about it. You probably visit hundreds of bathrooms in your lifetime. When bathrooms are the topic people are cynical at first, but many find they have much more to say than they ever imagined.

Skip wrote about the differences between the bathrooms he had visited in other countries. Noreen described how, in restaurants, she noticed a correlation between the restroom decor and the quality of the service. The other members of their writing group were drawn in by these observations. Both writers brought us beyond the superficial way of seeing a place.

TODAY write about bathrooms. You can describe particular ones you recall, explain etiquette in public bathrooms, detail how you would redecorate your personal bathroom, or simply free-associate on the page.

Ideas have come from the
strangest places.
J O Y C E   C A R O L   O A T E S

H O L I D A Y

Every now and then it is good to take an unexpected break.

You have been granted one day by the federal government to declare as a holiday. What will you name it? What is being honored? How is this holiday celebrated? Which businesses stay open and which close? What doesn't happen on this day? Be as whimsical, cynical, humorous, serious, or outrageous as you can.

THE PLOT THICKENS

A LOT OF PEOPLE tell me they have trouble developing plot. In writing classes you are taught a formulaic progression like Frietag's triangle: ground situation (a little girl lives across the woods from her grandmother), dramatic vehicle (her grandmother is ill so the girl brings her a basket of food), conflict (on her way she encounters a wolf), rising action (the wolf disguises himself as the grandmother), climax (the wolf tries to eat the girl), and denouement (the woodsman saves her, and they have supper), or the formula Alice Adams sometimes follows in a short story, ABDCE: action (get the reader involved), background (supply character's background), development (create drama and tension about something character cares about), climax (bring tension to a head and show that character is changed), ending (give a sense of character now—what is left, what the experience meant).

These are useful formulas, but they don't help you connect with the rhythm of your personal storytelling—whether you revel in suspense, description, internal dialogue, conflict—which impacts how your plots unfold. There is a great deal of difference between the way a plot of Alice Walker's and a plot of Ernest Hemingway's progress.

Once you recognize your narrative rhythms, you can hone them or even challenge them.

TODAY relate the same event three times, in one sentence, one paragraph, and one page. Notice how the event changes as you alter the amount of space you give it.

I tell a story the way some people eat an
Oreo cookie.
B. E. ZALMAN

SEX APPEAL

RASHIDI ASKED PAM for comments on his erotic poems. Pam said the voice was too distant. She meant that the poems didn't speak explicitly about sexual acts. Pam's comment said more about her preferences than Rashidi's poems.

When you write about anything you stand some distance from it, even when you speak from an "I" position. As both readers and writers we prefer a particular proximity to our subjects. And our preferences sometimes change. It's like sex appeal—physical charm that attracts. Some of us feel most attractive in form-fitting or revealing clothes. Some of us enjoy the subtle tension of implication and suggestion. Others like to create illusion. So it is with writing.

So it's not automatically better to be close to your subject. In Kazuo Ishiguro's novel *The Remains of the Day,* the narrator, who is recounting his own life, keeps a great distance from his story, which is full of highly charged and deeply emotional feeling.

TODAY write about sex. Start as far away as you can. As you write, gradually get as close as you can. You might begin with a topic that feels void of erotic or sensual energy. Trust the act of writing to move you toward the sexual. Another way to approach this study is to start as close as you can and gradually gain distance.

Sex can be renounced—but sexuality
cannot. We can't avoid sexual issues
by avoiding sex, or by dismissing
its importance, or by showing
disrespect to our own or other
people's sexual feelings.
SALLIE TISDALE

A Photographic Memory

WHEN YOU TAKE PICTURES on a trip, you look for images that will capture a feeling or the experience of what the place is like. Your photos don't document your journey, but they can evoke memories of it, first for you and then for others. The images will affect the traveler by recalling the actual experience, and the observer by suggesting it.

This is also true of writing. Poems, narratives, and dramas distill moments. You compose, freeze, and frame images and ideas.

Poets in particular will look to photography for inspiration. The richness of texture, story, and tone contained in a single image incite creative reinterpretation of it, a continuation, or its connection to another experience.

WRITE today so that each paragraph or stanza stands as its own photo. Consider whether the photo both works to recall something for you and stands on its own. Or, study a photo and either retell, extend, or connect to the image in words.

The moon develops creativity as chemicals develop photographic images.
NORMA JEAN HARRIS

BITE IN

Wʜᴀᴛ ᴀʀᴇ ʏᴏᴜʀ ᴀssᴏᴄɪᴀᴛɪᴏɴs with teeth? Food, flossing, vampires, your dentist, the first time a dog bit you? Run your tongue over your teeth. Those pieces of bone were your first tools. You still use them to cut, rip, tear, chew, grind. They are powerful. When we smile at each other we are displaying our built-in power tools.

Tᴏᴅᴀʏ begin with the word teeth *and keep on writing whatever comes up. When you are finished, read it over and highlight phrases or passages you would like to chew on some more.*

> Make the familiar exotic;
> the exotic familiar.
> Bʜᴀʀᴀᴛɪ Mᴜᴋʜᴇʀᴊᴇᴇ

H O W   T O

I T WAS ONE of those getting-to-know-you situations. Twenty of us were hired to teach gifted and talented eighth graders in residence on a college campus. The kids called it brain camp. On our first day the director of the program gave a talk on communication. He wanted us to play a game. The teachers partnered up. One of us got a pad and pencil and the other a drawing. I got a picture of a sailboat.

Without facing my partner and using only shapes and directions like up and down or right and left I had to get him to draw the sailboat. We had four minutes. My directions produced something that looked like a potted fern.

We writing teachers were thrilled. We knew what a great idea this would be if applied to writing. Writers don't get to peek at what the reader is seeing or experiencing. We put it out there as clearly and as powerfully as we can and then we have to let it go. Luckily, readers have imaginations. The most successful drawers in our game were the teachers who took a leap and began to draw what they thought was being described.

TODAY choose a simple action—riding a bike, making a bed, changing a tire—and explain how to do it, from beginning to end, without referring to what the action is. Whenever possible describe rather than name. For instance, if you choose making a bed, rather than refer to sheets, describe what they are, i.e., sixty-inch by eighty-inch rectangles of cotton cloth.

> I'd like to think that when I sing a song
> I can let you know all about the kicks
> in the ass I've gotten over the years,
> without actually saying a word about it.
> RAY CHARLES

Besides describing the concrete, physical world, creative writers explore the abstract one: how to love, how to attain freedom, how to face fear. You relate these experiences through the development of characters; you show instead of explain them to the reader.

Whether through humor, drama, or symbolism, characters often relate abstract conditions by failing at them. The writer reveals their failings and we learn from their mistakes.

TODAY pick an abstract concept: love, innocence, fear, freedom. Depict an aspect of this concept through you or your character failing at an incidental activity, such as organizing the contents of a closet or parking in a snowstorm without four-wheel drive.

> There are years that ask questions and
> years that answer.
> ZORA NEALE HURSTON

V I E W S   O F   V I O L E N C E

VIOLENCE IS A BIG FORCE better reckoned with than ignored. I for one cannot watch violent films no matter how brilliant the director or how important the subject. I wish I could because I feel like I'm missing something. But the times I've tried I feel despairing, terrorized, angry. The images can haunt me for years.

I can read violent passages in stories, poems, and plays as long as they aren't gratuitous. The impact is deep, the images stay with me, and I often cry as I read, but I don't feel randomly overwhelmed, helpless, or numb.

I know people who have a high tolerance for explicit violence and others who feel that viewing it is the only way to stay in touch with the state of the world. Each of us reaches our saturation point at different distances from this force.

In both film and literature violence can be portrayed through characterization rather than action; for instance, tone of voice, silence in the face of need, facial expressions, attitude, even the way a person eats. They bring the force of violence to light without sending the audience into shock. How you portray violence in your own writing reflects the ways it has the greatest impact on you.

*T*ODAY *portray violence in your writing using the methods that allow you to be the most detailed and specific in your description. Be absolutely thorough in illuminating this force.*

I probably have not killed anyone in
America because I write, I've
maintained good controls over
myself by writing.
S O N I A   S A N C H E Z

THE TRUTH IN ALL ITS FORMS

ONE DEFINITION OF TELLING the truth is to conform only to the facts. If you have ever listened to two sides of an argument you know that facts are subject to interpretation:

"I hate when you give me one of your 'how stupid can you be' looks."

"I didn't."

"You did. I saw it."

"I wasn't even thinking that."

"Well your face was."

"I didn't give you any look!"

"How can you say that? I saw your face; you didn't!"

Arguments like this neither improve communication nor make either person feel better. But they do point out that truth is rarely singular.

Your writings reflect *your truths,* what you know from the experiences of your life. If your life is anything like mine, those truths don't fall into neat categories; they are subject to revision, and some of them conflict. This is also a reflection of life. The painful truths you know are the ones which help you develop your villains.

MAKE a list of truths, one for every year of your current age. Or, narrate one brief incident from three different perspectives, thereby causing three different truths. Or, develop a character sketch for a villain based on a painful truth you've experienced.

There is no "the truth," "a truth"—
truth is not one thing, or even a system.
It is an increasing complexity.
ADRIENNE RICH

OVERHEARD

WRITERS NEED TO KNOW the story, even if it means making it up. For instance, if you are a member of your local art museum you probably receive invitations to the opening events. It's usually too crowded to view the new exhibit at these openings; but it's a terrific place to watch people and make up stories about them.

As you stroll through the gallery you will overhear snippets of conversation. Notice the array of clothing and the way people dance with each other. At my local art museum I have three favorite couples that I look for, adding to their stories each time they appear or fail to. You may be perceived as rude for staring, but it comes with the territory.

Other good places to pick up snippets of conversation are buses, subways, airports, and restaurants. I once read that Joyce Carol Oates carries a small notebook and will stop anywhere to take notes.

TODAY start with a piece of conversation you overheard. Continue the conversation down the page. Or, enter the conversation as a third party.

> I collect lines and snippets of things
> somebody might say— . . . then charac-
> ters begin to emerge.
> RICHARD FORD

P O S T C A R D S

THINK ABOUT POSTCARDS, both sending them and receiving them. There is the face of the card and that tiny square of space for a message, slightly odd because it's out of context, and subtly self-conscious because it's right out there where postal workers, the concierge, or a neighbor might read it:

Hi! We eat mangos for lunch, great views, Bréda's discovered her toes.

One of my favorite things to do in antique shops is read old post-cards with their inky curled script that's practically illegible and make characters and stories based on the people who wrote them.

When you feel stuck writing, elicit postcards. Use unlined index cards or draw rectangles on a piece of paper, draw a line down the mid-dle, address the right side to the character, narrator, or yourself and let the message roll on the left side. You don't have to send these cards through the postal system. But you can.

On your next trip, send yourself postcards—one every day you're away. If you travel with a companion ask him or her to do the same so you can compare them later. This assures you of getting interesting mail, reliving your trip at least once when you return, and not having to take a camera in order to have pictures when you get home.

TODAY try sending and receiving the directions you need for your current piece through postcards or postcard-sized messages and summaries. Or, whip off a post-card to five people you know from different areas of your life, including a relative, and notice the differences in tone or detail you choose for each reader.

I write letters to right brain all the time. They're just little
notes. And right brain, who likes to get little notes from me,
will often come through within a day or two.
SUE GRAFTON

J E A L O U S Y

I AM EITHER ONE of the most jealous people I know, or one of the more vocal about it. I hate it. Not only does it feel rotten but I can't ever feel only jealous. I also experience guilt and shame at the same time.

Whenever I come across anyone admitting to feeling jealous, especially writers, I am greatly relieved. Jealousy is such a taboo topic; we're more at ease discussing violence.

But jealousy has been a force in life from our beginnings. It is an emotion portrayed and explored in the earliest literature. It is an awful experience, one we've all had and will likely have again. But to probe jealousy in writing is to give a gift to the reader who feels unlovable and alone when it strikes; it may turn out to be a gift to yourself as well.

WRITE about jealousy today: tell a story about yourself; let jealousy work on one of your characters; write about someone you are jealous of; give jealousy a voice and let it speak for itself.

Green is the color of jealousy, but it is
also the color of hope.
J U L I A   C A M E R O N

TOURIST TOWN

IN NEW YORK CITY it's easy to spot tourists. They make eye contact, often smile, then quickly avert their gaze, remembering warnings about making eye contact with strangers in Manhattan.

Tourists are not in such a hurry either. If you observe them for a while (which rarely worries them, since it makes you look like a tourist, too, and not a very savvy one at that), you will notice that they look more intently at what is around them: their eyes are wider. Instead of filtering out distractions and focusing on their destination, they allow their surroundings in.

One of the reasons I love to travel is because it allows me to be in a state of being which is open to, and not protected from, my environment. As a tourist I walk in a different time zone where my purpose in looking is not to find my way but to let the way of a place touch me. Every day when I take my walk I try to be a tourist in my own town.

TODAY you are a tourist. The room you are now in is your hotel room. Look out the window or around the room and write about what you see, hear, notice.

The writer should never be ashamed of
staring. There is nothing that does not
require his attention.
FLANNERY O'CONNOR

I L L S ,   P I L L S ,
A N D   B I L L S

NOBODY WELCOMES ILLNESS. As a patient or a caregiver, your carefully made plans are disrupted. If the illness is chronic, life-threatening, or terminal it moves in and becomes an uninvited member of the household: tolerated, respected, resented, and occasionally reve-latory.

Dire illnesses bring you nose to nose with your spirit and force you to become more than what you were before their appearance in your life. It's scary, devastating, and painful. It also has its moments of humor, intimacy, courage, and holiness.

Even when you're the caregiver, illness plays on your psyche, pushes your limits. The first time I took care of a loved one (recovering from an appendicitis operation), I was on the phone in tears to friends every night, overwhelmed by what a big job it was and what a bad nurse I was.

Then there is the experience of being the sick one: ignoring the symptoms, waiting in the doctor's office, getting slayed by a head cold, attempting to get a comprehensible explanation of the statements from the insurance company. No matter who you are in this world or what you own, illness visits, and your characters will get sick too.

TODAY explore the subject of illness. Discover how one of your characters handles it. Or, select a moment from a personal experience of being sick or being a caregiver. Notice your perspective: is the incident humorous? poignant? clinical? dark? What means did you choose for writing: description? dialogue? narration of the event?

Writing involves a commitment greater
than illness.
BERNARD MALAMUD

The Heir Apparent

M Y MOTHER TELLS this story about a trip we took to France when I was three. She tells it to everyone. Not really *everyone,* but until I was about thirty it felt that way.

We were having dinner at the home of my mother's college friends, and at the end of the meal we were served bowls of fresh berries for dessert. Before I ate my berries, I poured a glass of champagne over them. As my mother tells it, the rest of the company was charmed and followed my lead. The point of the story, my mother explains, is how sophisticated and worldly I was even at three.

I can't tell whether my image of this event comes from my own memory or my mother's repetition of the story. In any case, I am the main character, my mother the narrator. But as with any family story, there were other perspectives. What did my father experience? What did our hosts see?

During the same trip, we were dining at a fancy restaurant and I picked up a wine glass and bit into it. This created quite a stir and I was whisked to the bathroom where my mother and the attendant worked to remove glass from my lip with tweezers. So much for sophistication.

What made me bite the glass? Were my parents arguing? Did I think the glass was candy? As writers we can take the familiar and turn it over a few times to discover and tell a different story.

T O D A Y choose a familiar family story and shift the focus. If the incident is about what happened to your Aunt Liz at last year's Thanksgiving dinner, retell the events from the perspective of Cousin Marty. Your new protagonist can relate his version of the event or he may decentralize the event, turning it into a passing experience as his own story unfolds.

Nostalgia is a seductive liar.
G E O R G E B A L L

S E A S O N S

Y OU ARE A PASSENGER in a car. One of your traveling companions says, "Wow, look at that view!" You look. What do you see? Not the same thing as your friend. Oh sure, you see a mountain range, sky, carpets of wheat fields, even the lone hawk between two clouds, but what saddens you is the deep green in the trees and what makes your friend gasp is how the sun funnels light into the valley.

The wise adage "Show, don't tell," reminds us to use concrete and specific details rather than abstractions to describe a place. But we need another adage to go with it: "Evoke, don't reconstruct."

Evocative descriptions of places don't rely on the obvious. Insist on the authentic detail that grabbed you. Don't settle for the familiar one.

TODAY pick your favorite season. First, recall a personal moment during the season. Then focus on only the details that evoke that experience. Use texture, smell, and sound if appropriate. Be truer to your response to the moment than to its features. Notice whether you start with specific features and move to general ones, or the other way around.

> . . . There are nuances that *scream louder*
> than the thing that's obvious.
> L O U I S E   N E V E L S O N

Turn the Page Upside Down

THERE ARE DAYS WHEN you just can't do it. I don't mean the ones when you are exhausted after long, intense periods of writing when what you really need is to participate in the physical, communal realm of your life. I mean the days when you want to be writing and either nothing comes out or it is so awful that lowering your standards would place you below the last circle of hell.

After you complete your litany of reasons why you've been fooling yourself into believing you're a writer, you have to find the hard-won, scratchy voice of sanity: lighten up!

Go for one of the pithy ideas I offer folks to help them loosen up (who is it who said we teach what we have to learn?). One is to break out of the confines of margins and lines. Turn your paper sideways and write right over the lines like a runaway trolley car. Divide your paper into three or four columns so that you can only compose a phrase or partial sentence on each line. Or, turn the page upside down.

Changing the orientation of the page may not change your writing, but this mild act of rebellion can trick the rational and critical mind into believing that you're no longer seriously attempting to write something good. So it eases off, looks for something else to scrutinize, and you can return to the joy of writing.

TODAY make columns or turn your page on its side and fill up the page. Do this even if you aren't having trouble getting started, so that when you do get stuck you'll have a visceral memory of this back door through which to escape.

One learns by doing a thing; for though
you think you know it, you have no
certainty until you try.
SOPHOCLES

P R A Y E R

WRITING IS A FORM of prayer. Even if you don't believe in a higher being, writing is prayer because it is a practice in words of offering, adoration, supplication, complaint, thanksgiving, and entreating. And, like prayer, writing follows a form.

How many times have you read a passage that has altered your state? I don't mean changed the way you thought because of the content of the passage, but rather by the choreography of rhythm and imagery, like a chant or the beat of a drum, lulled you and carried you deeper into yourself?

Not all writing is, or should be, reverent. But all strong writing makes a request of the reader, sometimes in an extremely subtle way. Powerful writing speaks out and moves us.

TODAY be aware of the prayer in your words. You might actually compose a prayer. Or, you might begin or revise a piece with an ear to the rhythms of prayer you are familiar with. If you work this way, begin by tapping out the beat of the prayer several times before writing.

Art is not a pastime but a priesthood.
JEAN COCTEAU

FORESHADOWING

FORESHADOWING: THAT LITERARY term you had to memorize the meaning of and then identify in novels in the ninth grade. Remember the first time you realized a fortune cookie had foretold something that eventually happened to you? For at least a second you reconsidered the way the world operates. It happens repeatedly in life; we look back at an event or a conversation and a clue to what unfolded becomes clear.

Omens are clunky in writing when they appear for no reason other than to alert the reader to what will happen later. The ones that work weave seamlessly into the narrative without calling attention to themselves; they are as subtle as the foretellings that appear in our lives.

Omens are believable in writing when they reflect those intuitive moments when a statement or an image strikes you as an impending truth. Normally, you dismiss the event or make a mental note to pay attention to whether it pans out, and then, like your characters, you go on about your business.

TODAY consider a situation that you had an intuition about. Go over the details of the situation to pinpoint what took place that clued you in. Speculate, in writing, on the unfolding of events that led up to the realization of your hunch.

The future enters into us in order to
transform itself in us, long before
it happens.
RAINER MARIA RILKE

B E   A   S P O R T

BALLS, FIELDS, NETS, arenas, sticks, helmets, uniforms, teams, points, goals, sports are favorite national pastimes that not only entertain and engage us but fill our language with metaphors. You can *strike out* at the shopping mall, be categorized as a *team player* at work, make *a pass* at someone you're attracted to, *run with* a good idea or *hit the mark* with it. Even if you aren't a fan you probably use some sports metaphors when you speak without even realizing it.

Sports, like types of writing, have their particular rhythms. Basketball and baseball proceed at different paces. So do novels and poems. Although each sport requires skill, the types of skills and strategies vary. So it is with writing, for instance, a play and a short story. Certain skills will overlap, like using dialogue, though it may be a more pronounced element in one form than in the other. As a writer you may also see yourself as a particular type of athlete: a pitcher, a goalie, an archer, a figure skater.

*T*ODAY *use as many sports metaphors as you can to describe an experience such as shopping for a car. Then describe the same experience and replace the sports metaphors with another category such as dance (side-stepping, waltzing, leading, following, leaping) or food (half-baked, digest, swallow, stew, meaty, gel, fishy). Or, describe yourself as a writer in terms of a particular sport and/or position in the sport. Or, use the word* sports *as a diving study for two full pages.*

> Poets are like baseball pitchers. Both
> have their moments. The intervals are
> the tough things.
> ROBERT FROST

ALTARS

WHAT SURROUNDS YOUR WRITING surface? Do you sit near a window? What objects and images sit with you or hang within view? Look at them now. They help you enter your writing and stay there. They are what make up your writing altar. There isn't anything New Age or cultish about it. Everyone creates altars out of what they value, including your Uncle Walter in Miami with his bowling trophies and pictures of his grandkids up on the mantel, including your characters and the narrators of your poems and essays.

Closets house altars and so do the tops of dressers and living room hutches. I keep an altar in my purse because I travel so much: three stones, a seashell, a Brazilian Figa, two gift enclosure cards, a fortune from a cookie, and a miniature padlock key.

DESCRIBE an altar today. It can be one of yours, a character's, or a friend's. What do the objects on the altar signify? What do they reveal about their owner?

Look for a long time at what pleases
you, and longer still at what pains you.
COLETTE

VERB VOLTS

VERBS ARE HIGHLY CHARGED. They are tools of craft and imagination. A man in one of my journaling workshops once said that he wanted to start a journal because he believed humans are verbs, not nouns. Another time, a friend complained to me that he wanted to be a human *being,* not a human *doing.*

Understanding resides with verbs. During a rehearsal of one of her pieces, the Japanese choreographer Kei Takei stopped our interpretation of her dance movement depicting workers in a field. With great compassion, she explained that in her country people *liked* to work. In that moment, my understanding of work was altered forever.

TODAY take a piece of paper and fold it in half lengthwise. Keep the paper folded, list eight nouns down the page. Do this now, before reading on. Now, choose any activity you are familiar with: basketball, gardening, writing, eating, sunbathing, sleeping. With the paper still folded, turn it to its blank side and list fifteen verbs that describe the activity; basketball might include dribble, pass, dunk, shoot. Now, unfold the paper and connect the verbs to nouns from your first list in surprising ways. Let one or more of these combinations serve as an image to begin a piece of writing.

The noun of the self becomes a verb.
STEPHEN NACHMANOVITCH

L I G H T S ,   C A N D L E S ,   A C T I O N

Remember the sensation of sticking your fingers in melted candle wax and feeling the wax dry on your skin? What else do candles bring to mind? Seances, birthday cakes, romantic evenings, old flames, the last power failure? Candles are prominent objects during Hanukkah, Christmas, Kwanzaa, Duwali. They create a palpable change in atmosphere. Now that we have electricity, most of the ways we use candles are symbolic. They evoke something abstract: an emotion or a state of mind.

My friend Julie makes a habit of sitting alone in her living room with a burning candle before she makes any major life decisions. She uses this time to imagine what each choice would feel like. The candle plays a major role in her contemplation because its light alters the tone of the room.

LIGHT a candle. Watch it for a while. Be aware of how the atmosphere changes. Notice your breath and the texture of the room. Write for a while. Blow out the candle. Now, notice the room again and write some more. Or, free-associate about candles for at least one page.

It doesn't have to be a big fire. A small
blaze, candlelight perhaps . . .
R A Y   B R A D B U R Y

SECRETS

T HE TOPIC OF SECRETS changes the atmosphere in a group. Folks become silent, lean back or forward in their seats, cock their heads, focus their eyes downward. Some people fiddle with their sleeves or the edges of their papers.

People expect me to ask them to confess to a horrible truth. But that isn't the purpose of the study. Secrets are a good place to explore the hidden in writing. They aren't always shameful; sometimes you don't mention the trip to New Guinea you're considering to friends and family because they're sure to dissuade you.

As soon as information attains the status of a secret, it becomes more desirable. Our natural curiosity is piqued.

Secrets are also those pieces of knowledge you believe will better your life. We look to philosophers, writers, poets, and elders when seeking those secrets, but often they are revealed in the ordinary workings of a day.

IN literature, secrets are uncovered, discovered, confessed, and developed. Today write about a secret. Choose one of yours or your character's. Or, write about a secret you have discovered that has improved an aspect of your life: the secret to making good soup stock or the secret to writing a resume; examine the secret for how it relates, as a metaphor, to your values.

There are certain mysteries, certain
secrets in my own work which even I
don't understand, nor do I try to do so.
GEORGES BRAQUE

IMAGINED SECRETS

WHEN I WORK on creative writing with young people I ask them to describe an object from nature and end the portrait with what they believe to be the object's secret. My favorite so far is Norman's cedar tree who is secretly ashamed of wooden houses.

The secrets you imagine arise from a combination of your creativity, intuition and curiosity. Have you ever been touched by a stranger or someone you have just met in a way that enables you to sense their secrets? Your intuition picks up on something that sparks your curiosity and imagination. For a writer, this is a calling to explore.

TODAY begin with an imagined secret. It can be a secret one character imagines another character is hiding, the secret of an object in nature, or a secret you sense about someone you have encountered. Let your intuition guide you through the secret and beyond.

A hunch is creativity trying to tell
you something.
FRANK CAPRA

VALUES AND BELIEFS

Your CHARACTERS AND NARRATORS hold your beliefs and values. You have to trust your characters. Even if their values appear to conflict with yours, they are still ideas that come from you. But what you value and what you believe are not synonymous with your longings and your wishful thinking. In strong writing you put aside the message, which may be profound, for the sake of the messenger—your characters, who have blisters on their feet, a whopping migraine, and a powerful thirst from carrying the message across the page.

No matter how profound your message is, it is usually not as compelling to a reader as the characters delivering it. For better or worse, ultimately we respond to people more than ideas.

TODAY consider what you value and know, from experience, to be true. Make a list. Now, make another list of what you once valued and believed to be true, but no longer reflects your current understanding. Develop a character sketch from each of these lists, or begin a dialogue in the voice of the speaker of each list. Either way, focus on bringing out the personalities of the speakers instead of their beliefs.

A bird does not sing because it has an
answer—it sings because it has a song.
CHINESE PROVERB

Critical writers hunt down ideas, take
them home and kill them. Creative
writers make love to ideas.
CORNELIA NIXON

IT'S ALWAYS US

ONE OF THE FACTS of creative writing is that you expose yourself. It isn't that all good writing is confessional, telling the specific details of your life; it's beyond that. You reveal your soul, you articulate your understanding, your view, your vulnerabilities, the aspects of yourself and your community that you may not be especially proud of.

You can only write from where you are at this moment, who you have become and what you understand so far in your life. Sometimes it's hard to work on a piece you're close to. You need time to gain perspective so you can see more of the picture. "The truth" changes as you change and gain experience. The process of writing is an exploration of who you have become.

It can be a struggle to get to that authentic voice; we are hardwired to forget our pasts, avoid powerful emotion, look forward and ahead. It is an effort to work against that current. The gift of writing is being the creator and created at once.

TODAY write about some quality in yourself you are not proud of. Remember, you don't have to write about yourself: You can write about how one of your characters feels about this quality; you can let the quality speak for itself; you can describe its effects on others.

> I hit my head against the wall because I
> don't want to know all the terrible
> things that I know about. I don't want
> to feel all these wretched things, but
> they're in me already. If I don't get rid
> of them, I'm not ever going to feel
> anything else.
> NTOZAKE SHANGE

S O U P F O R B R A I N S

A MAN ONCE ASKED me how to write when he had soup for brains. Good question. Go with the soup. We all have days when we can't express a solid image or thought. This is not the time to run down the street to pick up a carton of milk or review your appointment book. Some folks may pull one of their all-time favorite books off the shelf and read at this point for inspiration. Some of them end up reading instead of writing.

When you feel you have soup for brains, most often it is because you come to the page with a preconceived idea of what you want to accomplish and it isn't working. But there is nothing wrong with soup; it is a comfort on cold and dreary days. Rather than waste too much time and energy bemoaning your predicament or reveling in your frustration, focus on what you *can* accomplish: edit a different piece, work on another section, puke up your monthly allotment of terrible writing; there is always something to do. Even resistance eventually gives.

TODAY write without any preconceived ideas. Muck around in a piece that has been troubling you. Start a new piece. Or, return to a finished piece you are pleased with and explore the subject again starting with the phrase "Part Two."

Learn to trust your own judgement,
learn inner independence, learn to trust
that time will sort good from bad—
including your own bad.
D O R I S L E S S I N G

ORIGINAL VS. UNIVERSAL

THERE IS NOTHING NEW or original to be said in writing. Trust me on this. It has all been said before many times. So why write? Because the subjects, ideas, and themes we write about are essential, universal, fundamental, and necessary to explore and be reminded of.

Maybe what you have to communicate hasn't been mentioned in a while, or it hasn't been revealed in your particular voice, or it has been said in your voice but it didn't sink into people's consciousness the last time around so it needs to be voiced again. Maybe the only way you are going to take it to heart is if you say it yourself.

You become paralyzed by attempting to be original. You become genuine when you accept your place in the currents of universal concerns. And if you are writing away and an original thought rises, proving me wrong, terrific! I look forward to the new material.

TODAY look through your work and make a list of the universal concerns that appear. Notice what you write about again and again. Return to a theme you have touched on only a couple of times. Or, begin a piece that explores one you haven't yet tackled.

> There are only two or three human stories, and they go on repeating themselves as fiercely as if they had never happened before.
> WILLA CATHER

T R A N S L A T I O N S

WRITING IS AN ACT of translation. Our choice of words affects the meaning of what we say. Looking at translations of a work is the best way to make this important point clear. Consider the first line of "Caedmon's Hymn," which is believed to be the first piece of English literature and was discovered written in Old English:

> Nu sculon *h*erigean   *h*eofonrices Weard

These translations are by Albert S. Cook, Richard L. Hoffman, and George K. Anderson respectively:

> "Now must we hymn the Master of heaven"
> "Now let us praise the Keeper of the Heavenly Kingdom"
> "Now let us praise the guardian of Heaven"

Master, keeper, and guardian imply different perceptions and attitudes toward God. Whole religions and spiritual practices are based on these differences. As writers, we have a responsibility to pay attention to the words we choose. Not in the first draft of a piece, where it would paralyze us, but in the editing and revising of the piece. This is an integral part of the religion of writing; a thesaurus is one of our holy books.

TODAY return to a piece and revise it with an eye to making each word ring with accurate associations and connotations. Or, pick out some key words in a piece you are working on and make lists of synonyms for them. Use a thesaurus if you have one. If you don't, buy one today.

The poet's role, like the shaman of old, is to cross boundaries between the living and the dead, between this world and the other world. Translating is another way of crossing boundaries.

A N D R E W   S C H E L L I N G

SOUL FOOD

THIS IS A GREAT topic when you feel stuck, stopped, or blocked: new foods, favorite foods, ones you cannot stand. Eating is a universal, recognizable experience. Sharing a meal with another person has been a peacemaking ritual since the beginning of time. With a writer's eye, examine the menu descriptions at the next restaurant you visit; how do the descriptions of the food correspond to the tone and atmosphere of the place? Maybe you believe a person's food preferences are as important a characteristic as intelligence and kindness, or maybe, for you, food is an enemy.

Food and our relationship to it is telling. Even those who eat to live rather than live to eat are expressing an aspect of themselves and how they experience the world through their relationship to food. How do the characters you write about relate to food?

TODAY write about food. If this is too general a subject, begin by describing your most memorable breakfast, lunch, or dinner. Notice whether you spend more time describing the food, the atmosphere, or the company. Or, write the word food *at the top of the page and go wherever it takes you. Write at least three pages. Or, describe one of your characters eating or thinking about food.*

Grub before aesthetics.
BERTOLT BRECHT

WHAT I REALLY WANT TO SAY

WHEN YOU ARE WRITING along and after a few pages you still aren't getting at the words that quicken your breath, dry out your mouth, and make you lose all sense of place and time, you can reach a deeper, more authentic level by interrupting the part of your mind that is playing it safe, and give your guts a little room to speak out.

Interruptions are most effective when they are impolite. This emboldens the voice of truth looking for an opening. Give yourself the message: truth doesn't have to wait its turn. That can be enough encouragement to let it escape uncensored by propriety.

BEFORE you begin, mark the middle of your page. Then, start writing about any topic that interests you. Once you start, don't stop. When you reach the middle of the page, no matter what you're in the midst of, write the phrase "What I really want to say," and write whatever comes up until you fill the rest of the page. If the writing loses energy before you reach the middle of the page, use the phrase as soon as you notice the shift.

It always comes down to the same
necessity; go deep enough and there is a
bedrock of truth, however hard.
MAY SARTON

WILLING SUSPENSION OF DISBELIEF

THE WILLING SUSPENSION of disbelief is what occurs any time people enter a theater and accept the stage set as a real house or garden or mountaintop. In writing, the suspension of disbelief can be maintained as long as readers remain engaged in the events of the narrative and feel they have something at stake in the outcome. Creative writing doesn't always have to be realistic, but it does have to be plausible in the written world the writer invents.

TODAY begin by narrating, in one or two paragraphs, an ordinary event: walking your German Shepherd in the park, changing a tire on the interstate, canoeing on a lake. Next, describe the same event, only this time exaggerate the details. Now, write it one more time and make the event absurd. Notice how the focus of the piece changes each time and what you must do to effectively narrate the absurd.

. . . present

for inspection, "imaginary gardens
with real toads in them" . . .
MARIANNE MOORE

T E A C H I N G S

ONE OF THE BEST writing teachers is the natural world: Earth as teacher. The rhythms, cycles, and habits of the animal, vegetable, and mineral worlds offer us form and structure, patterns, lessons about timing and pacing, and a plethora of analogies to the human condition.

A writer notices the routine of a cat or the way sunlight progresses across a wall through the day and connects them to aspects of human circumstances. It might seem that always returning to our own condition is self-centered, even arrogant. But right up there with pleasure, communicating the human condition is the highest goal of writing.

How you connect to the teachers around you—the cat, the rain, the growing of celery—is in part what distinguishes your individual voice as a writer. It isn't just what you learn as you write, but also how you learn it.

TODAY make a list of some qualities that you or one of your characters aspire to: diligence, patience, compassion, fierceness. For each quality, describe and explain how one or two elements from the natural world embody the quality. Or, re-examine either your plot or your characters and find images from nature that embody them; for instance, your plot might gather like a storm or open like a tulip.

> Writing is more than just the making of
> a series of comprehensible statements: it
> is the gathering in of connotations, the
> harvesting of them, like blackberries in
> a good season, ripe and heavy, snatched
> from among the thorns of logic.
> F A Y   W E L D O N

Z Z Z Z Z Z Z Z Z Z 's

W<small>E SPEND ABOUT</small> a third of our lives asleep. Besides being a philosophical statement, this is also a fact of life. There are a number of theories about the realm of sleep, especially concerning dreams: are they the unconscious communicating, or the imagination taking over? Are they really not dreams at all, but wanderings on other planes of reality?

Watching people and animals sleep suggests that it is a pretty busy activity: we toss, turn, speak, walk, drool, kick, cry out. Sleep is another world.

Since it takes up such a large chunk of our experience of living, it is a topic worthy of exploring in writing.

W<small>RITE</small> about sleep. Describe your sleeping habits or your character's; describe insomnia; conjecture about what the realm of sleep is all about.

keep writing those deep questions sleep on
when you awake even you'll be gone
I K K Y Ū

A N   A U D I E N C E   O F   O N E

Even if you're unconscious of it, when you write a piece, you have an audience of one in mind. This is true not only for the poems and stories that begin with a dedication, but for any piece you create. The same person may be sitting in the mind's easy chair listening to every piece, or some one different each time. It's not that internal, critical voice that judges everything; it's the friend you love, a relative, a stranger you want to reach, for whose sake the piece comes into being. It may even be a part of yourself.

One way of moving deeper into a work is to invoke your audience of one, either by articulating to yourself who it is or by replacing the figure with a different one.

Today articulate who the audience of one is for your current work. Or, try writing another version of one of your pieces for a sole listener other than in the original. Or, imagine you have witnessed a car accident and describe it three times: to a police officer, to the mother of a child injured in it, and to your best friend.

It takes two to know one.
G R E G O R Y   B A T E S O N

GIFTS

WRITING IS A GIFT, both in the sense that it's a talent and that it serves as a present, first to ourselves and then to others. In Rebecca Brown's novel *The Gifts of the Body,* she reveals the sacred and beautiful aspects of caring for the dying. Her ability to communicate this, without sentimentality, is one of the gifts of this book.

As writers, we each have gifts: wit, an eye for detail, the ability to evoke place or era. Our characters and speakers also have their gifts.

TODAY write down your gifts as a writer. Then write down the way one of your characters is gifted. Now, use one of your gifts to write about one of your characters' gifts.

> The imagination conjures gifts; what
> the ungrateful, unsentimental part of
> the mind has to do is unwrap them . . .
> see them for what they are and then
> alter them.
> ROSE TREMAIN

THE SEDUCTION

WHEN I HEARD Natalie Goldberg speak, she said that writing is a seduction. I think she's right. The word *seduce* means, literally, to lead aside. Good writing captures our attention, persuades us, and tempts us to read on.

There are many methods of seduction: through mystery, by revealing, using charm, comfort or humor, by impressing, by being deferential. Whatever method you use, you are leading your readers away from the distractions and desires that call out in the physical world. So, along the way, you have to keep beckoning, keep making the experience powerful.

TODAY consider the ways you like to be seduced and to seduce others. Are they the same? Write using one of your favorite seductions, by being mysterious, charming, humorous, comforting. It isn't necessary to focus on the sexual; you can write about anything this way.

> What I was resisting, of course, was the
> seduction upon which writing rests.
> NANCY MAIRS

M A G N I F Y I N G   G L A S S

LIKE ALL THE ARTS, creative writing slows us down, requires us to look closer, deeper, longer, even as it quickens our pulse. Writing is a contemplation of what you are writing about. A piece communicates what the writer has culled from being willing to invest time and patience in the process of writing. We do it for the pleasure and reverence it stirs in us, and for the benefit of others who may be moved by our offerings.

Anyone might take a magnifying glass, microscope, or X-ray to an image or event, but it is the writer's commitment to take the time to record the vision *and* the experience of that vision. If you are in too much of a hurry, the writing suffers.

TODAY *write slowly. Start with a magnifying glass or a microscope focused on the subject of your piece and then use an X-ray machine.*

—in a way nobody sees a flower—
really—it is so small—we haven't the
time—and to see takes time . . . So I
said to myself—I'll paint what I see—
what the flower is to me but I'll paint it
big and they will be surprised into taking the time to look at it—I will make
even busy New Yorkers take time to see
what I see of a flower.
GEORGIA O'KEEFFE

C U T   A N D   P A S T E

When computers replaced typewriters (for most of us; fiction writer Stephen Dixon admits to writing on an old manual), I was excited. I still compose first drafts on lined yellow legal pads, in spiral notebooks, and on the backs of old photocopies, but the computer gave me another means of applying my favorite revision technique: cut and paste. When I discovered the commands on my computer software actually use these terms, I was thrilled.

Despite the cut and paste function keys, I often return to the old hard-copy method for the same reasons I begin drafts in longhand. There is value in the physical relationship: touching the words on paper. It just works better sometimes. The shuffling and moving around stimulates the synapses in a fresh way.

TODAY take a piece you are working on, cut or tear the paper into separate paragraphs or stanzas, and assign each one a number or letter. Treat a dialogue as one paragraph. If you're working on a play, cut or tear each time the speakers change or the same speakers switch topics. Shuffle the order of the piece's components, considering each of the possibilities. If more than one sequence intrigues you, note each of them. Paste down each new sequence, or make a copy of each version using the computer. Continue to write from one of the new possibilities.

> The beauty of word processing, God
> bless my word processor . . . The prose
> becomes like a liquid that you can
> manipulate at will.
> SUE GRAFTON

T I M E   o n   O u r   S i d e

Time is relative in writing. A single event can span an entire novel or three words.

Your writing habits and rhythms also relate to time and your temperament. If you're the type that flits back and forth between projects you can still work on a consistent basis, but you will define consistency differently than those who sit down to write, look up, and find that six hours have passed.

I work in two-hourish spurts. I may write twice or three times a day or only once. This is the rhythm that works best for me. If I don't have hours, I take twenty minutes. Often these mini-sessions are as productive as the longer ones.

On certain days you may only have a few minutes to reread a piece, pencil in hand, but something valuable may come of it. You can also think in tasks rather than in time. For instance, write with the task that you will create new material for a poem, or finish another section of an essay, or spend several pages with a particular character. If you don't stick with the task you've set because another piece is on your mind, switch gears, but still give yourself direction: generate more material, reshape, work on the timing.

Today experiment with time. Extend or limit the time you devote to revising a piece. Or, if possible, write during a different time of day than usual. Or, set yourself an achievable task and meet it.

> I give people time so they feel their
> lives moving over their skins.
> JENNY HOLZER

R E A D I N G   A N D   W R I T I N G

MOST OF US WRITE because we love to read. You have to love words and what they do to you to want to spend so much time wrestling them. Books make love to us; we want to make love back. Books speak the truths we suspect. They take us into a realm that only art can open, and send us back to our world refreshed. They are mentors; they initiate us.

Some of us read a book and feel called to join the conversation from the writer's end. Many writers I know can name the writers that first called them. For me it was Emily Dickinson, then Rainer Maria Rilke, T. S. Eliot, Grace Paley, Philip Levine, and Ntozake Shange; then the list gets unwieldy. Each of these writers invited me. I've been fortunate to actually speak to some of these writers face to face, but that wasn't how their invitations came. It was through reading their work.

In my twenties I had convinced myself to bag writing altogether and go to social work school. I'll never forget this: I picked up a book of Grace Paley's short stories and started to read. My face heated up and I had to take deep, deep breaths. I put the book down and began to cry. Then I did something that, at the time, I thought was pretty weird; I got out my journal and channeled Grace Paley. Well, not really; I wrote a letter to myself from her. It told me to keep writing. I briefly worried over my mental health and then got back to work.

TODAY remember a writer who called you to write. Write a letter to them about either how they called you or where you are as a writer today. You don't have to send it. Or, let one of the writers who called you send a letter to you.

Many of us write because we are readers and have grown up in a long tradition, and we want to be able to add to that extraordinary flow of interpretations of the world.
R O S E L L E N   B R O W N

MIRRORS AND REFLECTIONS

A MIRROR IS NOT only a surface that reflects an image of what is in front of it. Any creature or object can be a mirror, meaning it can reveal an aspect of our condition. Pieces of writing serve as mirrors which, like the conventional versions, distort an object in order to reflect it. The verb to reflect comes from the Latin *flectere* meaning "to bend." Bending an image might include exaggerating it, leaving out parts of it, depicting it from an unusual angle. For instance, a photographer might move the furniture in a room closer together to compensate for the way a wide-angle lens adds space to the image.

Mirror comes from the Latin *mirari,* "to wonder." So another aspect of the relationship between writing and a mirror is showing an image in a way that incites awe. It's up to you to determine the amount of distortion necessary to make the written experience throw back the real-life one.

TODAY bend an image to make it reflect a particular mood. Or, work the image of a mirror into a current piece so that it becomes a source of wonder rather than resemblance. Or, write about an experience you recall involving a mirror.

Any idea, person, or object can
be a mirror.
HYEMEYOHSTS STORM

W O R D   W A T C H

A YALE STUDY reported that the twelve most persuasive words in the English language are save, money, you, new, health, results, easy, safety, love, discovery, proven, guarantee. I could go on a diatribe about the implications this has about the state of our country, but I won't. However, you should feel free to use this information as the springboard for impassioned social commentary in an outraged or humorous vein.

The study is a reminder that we each have strong responses to certain words though our responses may not be the same. The actor and playwright Anna Deveare Smith recounts a college assignment, which was to write an essay about a word that had deep significance to her. She and the only other Black student in the class both chose "nigger," though for one it was a dreadful epithet and for the other a word of power. Spoken or written words spark nerves.

We all carry around words that are charged for us. For writers, the words may strike us as much for their sound and texture as for their meaning. Some words fire our souls, others feel good in our mouths. In a final draft, choose your words with all of this in mind.

TODAY make the following personal lists of twelve: the most terrifying or dangerous words, the most beautiful words, the most annoying words. Words from these lists might be the subjects of poems, essays, or stories. You might pick one and explore it further in an acrostic (see p. 107 for explanation of an acrostic). Or, choose one word that gets to you and use it as a diving study.

> I think of the self that I write about as being made out of words. He's been reconstructed constantly, over and over again, out of words.
> CHARLES WRIGHT

RECYCLABLES

Writers are recyclers. Turning an item into something that is useful in another way is part of what writing is all about.

We have an aversion to secondhand material in this country. We are constantly encouraged to replace what is usable with something new and therefore allegedly better, despite the fact that the workmanship of older items is sometimes superior.

You have a resource you might neglect due to this unfortunate attitude. The use of found material such as headlines, fortune cookie messages, scraps of conversations, news items can stimulate you to stretch both your style and subjects. Reinterpretation of a popular tale is another form of recycling, like turning *Romeo and Juliet* into *West Side Story.* And finally, using images and lines from your previous work in a current piece can foment a powerful experience.

Auguste Rodin reproduced several of his pieces in various mediums and sizes over his career. The songwriter Sting repeats a line from a previous ballad in a newer one creating an echo that infuses the new song with an additional layer of associations.

Today experiment with recycled or secondhand material. You might use a headline or news item in a narrative or poem; reinterpret a well-known narrative; or, weave a particularly compelling image or line from your previous work into a current piece.

Influence seems to me a peculiar prohibition in the West.
It's like a capitalist influence in art, the idea that each person
is supposed to produce a totally unique commodity. But
we're all in a common language and a common culture. I
don't see why each of us has to think of our own
particular territory of subject matters, themes, or styles
as if we were each locked in a closet.

Lyn Hejinian

B E A U T Y   A N D   I N J U S T I C E

T HE WORLD IS unforgivingly inconsistent and complex. This is another reason why we write. Otherwise it's too overwhelming to move
through the braids of beauty and injustice. We are grateful for the
beauty which soothes, heals, and strengthens us, but it is interwoven
with the injustice that binds us to a difficult path. Writing is part map,
part inventory of the road.

Beauty and injustice exist side by side, as well as completely intertwined. They are at odds in much of literature. We always come back to
writing about them attempting to understand or clarify their relationship.

*TODAY create a piece in which beauty and injustice exist side by side. You may
concentrate on one incident or list several. Or, work on a piece in which the two
are intertwined. Or, read over some of your current work with an eye to where
you address these themes and how they interact. In choosing any of these, notice
whether your focus is on the personal or the communal. Later, experiment some
more with whichever was less prevalent.*

Great writing can be conjured by
great injustice.
L A N C E   M O R R O W

OUT OF LOVE

SINCE CREATIVE WRITING is an act of love, it is impossible not to be, in some sense, always writing about love. Because of its overarching presence in almost all writing, aspects of love don't have to be the central subject of any given piece. Love shows up in one form or another anyway. But this is not a reason to ignore love as a theme. Rather, it is a reason to understand what aspects of it you are touching in any given piece and what you are communicating about it.

Think about the many ways we speak metaphorically about love: as madness—she's crazy about him; as sorcery—the magic is gone; as energy—sparks flew between them; as a patient—let's try to revive our relationship; as war—he fled from her advances.

It will always be important to write about love because our understanding of it changes over time. The trick is to stay honest about the nature of whichever love you write about. You do everyone a disservice—both your characters and your audience—when you try to protect them from the chaos of it.

TODAY try writing about a type of love you don't often explore, such as platonic love, spiritual love, patriotism, or phileism. Or, review the last few pieces you've written and identify the types of love you include and what you have communicated about them. Then choose one and continue the thread in the same piece or a brand new one.

I don't think anything is the opposite
of love.
ANNE LAMOTT

MYTHS ARE MAGICAL: ancient stories that explain natural phenomena, beliefs, institutions, and practices. They are alluded to in many pieces of literature. These powerful tales speak to our souls. We generally reread them several times over a lifetime. If we are exposed to them early in life they influence our writing.

All myths involve elements of wonderworking. Many focus on the theme of creation: explaining how seasons came about or how the leopard became spotted. One reason myths endure is because they address the yearnings and challenges inherent in the human condition. In this way, myths are timeless and invite reinterpretation from contemporary perspectives.

I love reading reinterpretations of classic tales in which mythic figures speak about themselves. James Joyce, Margaret Atwood, André Gide, and Marion Zimmer Bradley are among the many who have created extraordinary versions of myths.

Myths can also supply you with models of plot sequencing, not necessarily to copy outright, but to use as a first thread.

*T*ODAY *invent a first-ever creation myth: the first kiss, the first birthday party, the first sunset; or, retell a favorite myth in a modern setting or by allowing secondary characters to tell it from their perspective; or, make a list of all the myths you can remember; or, reinterpret the meaning of a myth. Or, recall in detail the experience of hearing a particular myth for the first time.*

How far can a Greek goddess lead a
Black poet?
R I T A   D O V E

PANTOUM: DANCING
WITH FORM

FORM IS A MYSTICAL equation; it forces your hand the moment you invite it to the page. Writing within a predetermined structure helps you approach difficult subjects and steers the direction of the piece.

One of my favorites is the Malayan Pantoum. It is a poetic form in which all the lines in the poem repeat themselves. This means you are responsible for asserting every line twice; nothing new may be said without responding in some way to what has come before it. The poet Jane Shore wrote "Fortunes Pantoum," from Chinese cookie fortunes. I wrote a series of pantoums culled from graffiti. This one is a group effort by the students at North Dorchester High:

A lion in the cave	(1)
He hunts at night	(2)
What is this lion in a cave?	(3)
The king of all beasts	(4)
He hunts at night	(2)
Ruler of the forest	(5)
The king of all beasts	(4)
He is dangerous to catch	(6)
Ruler of the forest	(5)
Ruler of your heart	(7)
He is dangerous to catch	(6)
He is vicious and strong	(8)
Ruler of your heart	(7)
A lion in the cave	(1)
He is vicious and strong	(8)
What is this lion in a cave?	(3)

Writing a pantoum is a way to dance with form and let it lead.

TODAY try a pantoum. Each stanza is four lines long. Lines 2 and 4 of each stanza become lines 1 and 3 of the next. Now, don't panic! Number your page vertically in the following pattern: 1,2,3,4 2,5,4,6 5,7,6,8 7,9,8,10 9,11,10,12 11,1,12,3. Each line is assigned a number. You'll notice that in the last stanza the lines that didn't get repeated from the first stanza return. Hint: Write your first four lines and then copy them into their places in the other stanzas before continuing. Do this after each stanza. Hint: Line three is also going to be your last line. Hint: If you want your pantoum to be longer, just keep following the pattern, and in the final stanza bring back the unused lines from the first stanza as lines 2 and 4. Go on and try it—it's fun, really!

> The tougher the form the easier it is for
> me to handle the poem, because the
> form gives permission to be very
> gut-honest about feelings.
> MAXINE KUMIN

D R I V I N G   F O R C E S

WE ARE DRIVEN to write, but we are not all driven by the same things. We share a desire for understanding our relationships to the world and other people, but you may long to craft a seamless narrative while your writing buddy is urged forward by a belief in the interconnectedness of emotional states and the natural world.

Similarly, each of your characters and narrators is driven by one or more forces. Often their driving forces conflict, creating the reason to tell the story. After completing a first draft it is time to articulate the driving forces at play. In later drafts it is helpful to look at the way these forces are taking shape.

A story is also driven by one of three overarching elements: character, plot, or universe. *Tom Sawyer* is a character-driven novel; the focus is on what happens to Tom and how he develops. "Star Trek" is a universe-driven drama; although there are main characters, they exist and interact in order to demonstrate the state of the world around them. Agatha Christie mysteries are plot-driven; what happens next is most important.

What drives you?

TODAY concentrate on driving forces. Identify the forces that drive you to write or those that drive one or more of your characters; examine a current piece for driving forces, or make a list of your favorite stories or poems and identify which are character-, plot- and universe-driven in order to recognize which type of literature you are most attracted to.

Novels allow me to create a whole world.
NTOZAKE SHANGE

Character is the center of fiction for me.
ALLAN GURGANUS

VEGETAL LOVE

FRUITS AND VEGETABLES are as gorgeous as flowers. We all have our favorites. If you resist eating them, there are those that you are visually attracted to because they are an extraordinary color or their features are especially evocative or strange. Eating an artichoke or a persimmon is an intimate experience some prefer to engage in when alone.

Vegetables and fruits are bounteous subjects; visual artists render still lifes of them. People sow and tend them in back yards and windowsill gardens. Grocers proudly display them. We poke, prod, sniff, and devour them.

TODAY describe in minute detail a favorite fruit or vegetable. Begin with a physical description and allow it to go in whatever direction it wants to. Or, have a character you are working with do the same.

The creative mind plays with the object
it loves.
C. G. JUNG

RANTINGS AND RAVENS

FOR A LONG TIME I had a snobby attitude about Edgar Allan Poe. I was under the impression that he wasn't a "serious" writer. I'm not sure how I developed this attitude; it certainly wasn't from reading Poe and paying attention to my reaction. I was one of those souls slow to understand that my own opinion counted. I've made up for lost time by having plenty of opinions now.

When I read Poe in earnest I found much to admire. His famous poem "The Raven" inspired me to reconnect to the literary trope of the messenger bringing knowledge to a character. In Poe's poem, a raven appears at his door with the message "Nevermore."

When we speak of being inspired by the muse, we evoke the same image of visitation and divine communication. Most of us have experienced this at least once with writing: a piece that just emerges whole. It's astonishing. It is a divine rush to be the recipient of art, or anything for that matter, through visitation.

TODAY create a piece in which a contemporary speaker is visited by a raven or any other type of messenger. How does the messenger arrive? What is the message? How does the speaker respond? The piece may be serious or humorous. Or, write about a personal experience in which you were visited by some sort of messenger.

> . . . perhaps all the dragons of our lives
> are princesses who are only waiting to
> see us once beautiful and brave.
> RAINER MARIA RILKE

Aɴ ᴀʀᴛɪsᴛ ᴏɴᴄᴇ ᴇxᴘʟᴀɪɴᴇᴅ to me that the shapes made by the space around the objects in a piece were as important to the composition as the shapes themselves. It reminded me of one of the elements of writing that is unique to the art form: the ability to create an image by negating it.

If you describe someone as not friendly and not shy, or as not light-skinned and without pierced ears, a picture of the person begins to form through the aspects you choose to negate. Wallace Stevens uses this technique in the poem "Disillusionment of Ten O'Clock." When you use negation as description you also often reveal as much about the speaker as what is being described. Negation is an organic first approach to description. It parallels the real-life problem-solving method of discovering what we need by eliminating what we don't.

Tᴏᴅᴀʏ describe a person, place, idea, or object through negation. Or, describe yourself from the perspective of what or who you are not.

> The houses are haunted
> By white night-gowns.
> None are green . . .
> None of them are strange,
> With socks of lace
> And beaded ceintures.
> People are not going
> To dream of baboons and periwinkles.
> Wᴀʟʟᴀᴄᴇ Sᴛᴇᴠᴇɴs,
> ꜰʀᴏᴍ "Dɪsɪʟʟᴜsɪᴏɴᴍᴇɴᴛ
> ᴏꜰ Tᴇɴ O'Cʟᴏᴄᴋ"

Dear R:

I hope you are well. We're finally having clear weather here. I'm glad we're staying in touch during this intense period of work. Reading your letters and stopping to write to you are my main support for now. Bless the postal service.

Do your characters correspond? Letters were a popular form for novels in the eighteenth century. They are such an intimate means of disclosure. When I read a letter in a piece of writing it makes me feel as if I'm being admitted to a confidential space. Maybe that's why even form rejection letters sometimes seem personal. When I unfold a letter or seal one in an envelope and drop it into the metal box I'm momentarily overcome by possibility. The writer Shana Alexander said, "Letters are expectation packaged in an envelope."

Please send your thoughts on the enclosed essay.

As always,
B

TODAY use letters that you have received as material. Or, list the pending correspondence of one of your characters. Or, write a letter in your own or a character's handwriting.

> Many ideas grow better when they are
> transplanted into another mind than
> the one where they sprang up.
> OLIVER WENDELL HOLMES

C O L L E C T I O N S

Everyone collects. Whether or not a character's collection shows up, an exploration of it provides you with useful information. What a person collects, how he collects, and where he keeps it reveal aspects of his character.

We've all had some experience with collecting, however short-lived: guitars, artwork, earrings, cuckoo clocks, people. My friend Michael collects Fiesta Ware dishes that he acquires by getting up at four in the morning and driving to estate sales to be among the first to scope them out. My mother used to collect S & H Green Stamps and matchbooks, and she has one of the best collections of Sixties protest buttons I've ever seen. A friend's mother collects canned vegetables.

Some people collect unconsciously, deriving pleasure from owning rather than displaying. My mother collects deliberately and takes pleasure in mounting her buttons. My friend's mother hides her cans.

Today describe the eight most prized possessions in your collection or your character's. Or, describe the collection process and how it is housed. Whichever you choose to do, spend some time looking over what you have written and writing a bit more about how collecting corresponds to other aspects of the collector's life.

It takes a while for our experience to
sift through our consciousness.
N A T A L I E   G O L D B E R G

DRAMATIC MONOLOGUE

Rita Dove's poem "Parsley" is a dramatic monologue, a form of poetry in which the poet speaks in the voice of a person who is usually, but not always, from the past. In the first section, Dove speaks in the voice of one of the Dominican Republic's tens of thousands of Haitian cane workers; in the second section, she conveys the thoughts of the dictator Trujillo as he formulates their massacre.

Dramatic monologue is a study in creating character. One way of approaching such a piece emerged at a talk given by playwright and actor Anna Deveare Smith, when she explained a technique she learned to become her characters: finding the psychic space where she is neither herself nor the character.

In other words, since it isn't really possible to know how another person thinks and feels, rather than pretend to know, you write from the space between what you understand about the person and what you know about yourself. You write from the hallway between these two rooms.

Today try creating a dramatic monologue. Choose a figure you know fairly well. Prepare yourself by reviewing what you know about the person. Focus on a particular aspect of them that you experience as mysterious or peculiar. Now, see an image of the person standing a few feet away from an image of yourself. Recognize the space between the two of you and begin to write from this position.

We're looking into ourselves, looking at
the world around us, and letting our
monsters out.
LENORA CHAMPAGNE

THE DIRECTOR'S CHAIR

AFTER YOU GET the raw material down on the page, you have a lot of decisions to make about crafting it. It can feel overwhelming. This is when you sit in the director's seat. You make choices. You consider which strategies to use to make the scenes or ideas unfold for the strongest cumulative effect.

For instance, when describing a setting you can move from specific to general, general to specific, or alternate between them. The choice you make determines the emphasis and timing of the description and often the tone as well. Think of a movie camera filming what you've written. Is it more effective to open the scene with a close-up of a sweating glass of lemonade, then the bicycle helmet beside it, followed by the window overlooking Mount St. Helens, or is the tone of the scene better set by a pan of the apartment and then the close-ups on key props? The first draft of a passage may include all the elements you want to show, but often the order needs your director's eye. When a written passage feels off and you can't determine the reason, begin by reconsidering the placement of its elements.

TODAY think of yourself as a movie camera while writing a description of a setting. Or, write a one-paragraph description of setting starting with a general view of the scene and then moving to specific details. Next, describe the same scene from specific to general, and finally, alternate between them in the final version. Is the version that reads better to you the one you were more comfortable writing?

Creativity is really the structuring
of magic.
ANN KENT RUSH

CITIZEN WRITER

EACH OF US identifies with several communities at once: the community of a neighborhood, of parents, of social workers, of Buddhists. Because some of these communities overlap they influence one another and pose questions such as what it means to be a Buddhist parent.

When you are working at your desk or in your studio you live part-time in the realm of writing, but you don't stop being a member of several communities or a citizen of your country. How you experience your citizenship in your country in this century is reflected in the style and content of your work.

TODAY list all the communities of which you are a member. Cluster the ones that influence one another. What questions do these overlaps raise? Choose one and write in response to it. Or, write about being a citizen of your country right now, today. Or, compare two communities that you have been a part of in the past with an eye toward their similarities as well as their differences.

> No matter how individual we humans
> are, we are a composite of everything
> we are aware of. We are a mirror of
> our times.
> LOUISE NEVELSON

W I N D O W S

Windows admit light, and the stares of people; they are the spaces between the inside and outside worlds. Windows also present a limited view, and we speak of windows of opportunity. Do you consider television a window? What about photographs or mirrors, or literature?

TODAY free-associate about windows for one or two pages. Or, describe the view from the same window at different times of the day or by season. Or, describe a character or room as seen through a window.

> Life is denied by lack of attention,
> whether it be to cleaning windows or
> trying to write a masterpiece.
> N A D I A   B O U L A N G E R

TROUBLE WRITING

Just as you may have difficulty with particular studies in this book, so I had trouble articulating some of them. I didn't skip the ones that were harder to write. Did you?

We all have trouble writing sometimes. There may come a point in a piece when it is better just to let it go, come back to it later, or abandon it altogether. Generally, this happens when you lose interest in the subject or no longer believe what you are saying about it. This is different from reaching a point when writing the piece gets hard. That's the time to stay with it because you may be on the verge of a breakthrough in the piece or in relation to how you write.

Today start with a topic that is difficult for you and work with it for a while. Or, pull out a piece you are struggling with and spend some time with it. Or, return to a study in this book you skipped and do it.

It is not because things are difficult that
we do not dare; it is because we do not
dare that they are difficult.
Seneca

COLOR TREATMENT

ONE MAY AFTERNOON I walked in the park with my friend Caroline admiring the magenta-colored azalea bushes. She agreed they were stunning and explained that their color is the one shade of the spectrum the plant rejects, that it can't absorb. That's what color is, she mused.

It took several moments for it to sink in: *the color of a thing is the color it rejects, the one color it is not.* This struck me as an irony reflecting conditions in life, particularly in the area of personal relationships. The analogy prompted an epiphanous moment in my understanding.

TODAY make two lists: one of colors that attract you, and one of colors that repel you. Choose a color from each list. Approach each of them from your other senses; how do these colors sound, smell, taste, and what is their texture? Which images that emerge can you use in a current piece? Or, begin with the word color *and use it as a diving-off place. Or, write a poem or short piece in which every line or sentence mentions the same or a different color.*

> Painting is silent poetry, poetry is
> eloquent painting.
> SIMONIDES

C L I C H É

... To me there's something almost
slightly sacred about clichés, just because so many people have used them
to express strong emotions.
J O H N A S H B E R Y

You've probably been warned to avoid using clichés. This is excellent advice if you are describing a sunset, or a person, or if you are writing a poem that is serious in tone.

However, your characters might use a cliché here and there because it tells us something about them. Or you could put clichés in your narrator's mouth, signaling readers to question her perceptions.

The poet John Ashbery uses clichés in his poems because they are familiar and evocative. But he doesn't rely on them to carry the entire emotional weight of the poems, which are often infused with humor, irony, and wit.

What is important is that you be able to recognize a cliché. It is also important that you not use one rather than stretch your ability to express emotion. When you do use a cliché, use it deliberately.

SINCE it is important to recognize a cliché when one appears, today list as many of them as you can think of. Or, try using a cliché deliberately to develop a character or narrator. Or, pick a cliché and change one word in it. Write a piece using the revised cliché.

L E S S O N S

W HAT KIND OF LESSONS did you take as a kid? Whether your lessons were in piano, gymnastics, hunting, cooking, or car maintenance, returning to that time and your teachers is a rich source of material. The combination of your memories and your current perspective almost guarantees that a textured and emotionally rich piece will emerge. It is also an excellent study in which to experiment with shifting from one perspective to another because you move back and forth from your childhood perception to your current view.

TODAY make a list of all the lessons and teachers of those lessons you had as a child. Be creative in developing the list; it isn't necessary to limit the list to those lessons that took place outside the home, cost money, and came from a professional teacher. Choose one lesson to write about; you might describe your relationship to the teacher, what you learned, how you learned. Whichever you choose to focus on, spend some time in the twin realms of hindsight and adult perspective.

An essential portion of any artist's labor
is not creation so much as invocation.
L E W I S   H Y D E

O THE PAIN

Pain is important: how we evade it,
how we succumb to it, how we deal
with it, how we transcend it.
AUDRE LORDE

Migraine? Broken bone? Pulled muscle? Childbirth? Pain is a universal experience. A great motivator. Both the physical and emotional varieties are unavoidable in life and literature. The aspects of pain that Lorde points out determine the decisions and actions of all characters and creatures alike.

Do you or your characters deal with physical pain and psychic pain in a similar way? The various ways we handle pain can be at the core of conflict between people, between cultures, within a single person. Sometimes the process of writing is painful too. Use it. Capture the rhythms, sensations, and images that the pain creates.

It is said that if we didn't experience pain we wouldn't have art. I'm not sure I believe this, but art and literature are one place people go to learn how to endure pain.

TODAY write about pain or from pain. Approach pain through any one of the aspects mentioned. Attempt to stay with this topic for at least two pages, no matter how difficult it is. Or, consider how pain is motivating a character or speaker in a current piece. Or, write about the difference between pain you expect and experience with a purpose and the kind of pain that takes you by surprise.

THE DREADED SECOND DRAFT

DO YOU DREAD the second draft more than any other part of the writing process? In the first draft you're living in the center of pure creation. What reaches the page is new, developing in the moment, drawing on intuition, curiosity, emotion, and intellect. What you are attempting to portray is, if not clear, then fresh and urgent.

While in the first draft you're writing for yourself, in the second draft you begin to let go of the piece for the sake of what it can offer to others. Fears of not being able to translate the experience come up. You might doubt yourself.

This is the experience of many writers and why you are often advised to let a new piece sit for a while before you return to it. Time also allows you to reabsorb what you discovered in the first draft, and to contemplate the discoveries made through the *process* of writing. Then you can approach the next stage focused and with the first inch of objectivity necessary to begin crafting.

By the time you complete a second draft, you're committed to what you're attempting to communicate and you've gained some understanding of where it is and isn't working. The piece begins to become less precious, more distinct, with a soul of its own.

*T*ODAY *check where you stand in relationship to the piece you are working on (or a section of it). Ask yourself how much you have learned and gained from its creation up to this point. Notice at what distance you stand from the piece; have you received enough from the experience to communicate it to others? Or, write about the difference between the process of creation and the process of revision.*

First drafts are for learning what your
novel or story is about.
BERNARD MALAMUD

L Y R I C I N T E N T

W E LOVE STORIES. Most folks have a story to tell. But literature isn't only a narration. It is also a song. The lyric poem or passage is how your meditations and contemplations of events unfold in creative writing.

If you are one of the people who skip over descriptive passages so you can get back to the action, writing lyric passages will be as challenging for you as writing action and plot is for people who revel in descriptions of setting, food, and lovemaking.

A lyric passage or poem isn't fluff. Its function isn't to pad a story, build suspense, or provide a break in the action. Rather, like a melody it relates emotion, mood, and tone while evoking an aspect of the human condition. Your choice of words and rhythm of the sentences are the chords, bewitching and enchanting the reader more deeply into your written world instead of onward through it.

*T*ODAY *write a lyric piece. Begin by describing an object or emotional condition of a person for one full page. Next, reshape the passage to deepen it, paying attention to the music: the rhythm of the sentences, the choreography of the images, and the specific word you choose to name any given detail or action.*

> When a man does not write his poetry,
> it escapes by other vents through him.
> R A L P H W A L D O E M E R S O N

Naming a character takes the same consideration as naming a child. We choose baby names that speak to our hopes for who our children will grow into. When naming characters we highlight an aspect of them that is important to the story. Some writers go to great lengths researching the names they use, picking ones that have mythological or religious associations. The etymology of most names is a personality trait. Phillip in Greek means "lover of horses"; Elizabeth comes from a Hebrew word meaning "oath of God." Electra is from the Greek word for amber.

Some characters are born from your imagination already named. Others go nameless until the piece is nearly done. Either way, it's helpful to your understanding of your characters to look up the meanings of the names you choose.

A few of us are naturally gifted at inventing names. Henry James was brilliant at it: his characters included Henrietta Stackpole, Ralph Touchett, and Lavinia Penniman. The rest of us work at it.

The makers of ancient narratives attached epithets to the names of characters in order to emphasize their qualities: Wily Odysseus, Swift Mercury. Real people are so dubbed by history: Ivan the Terrible, Catherine the Great, Richard the Lionhearted. Giving characters a couple of epithets while working with them helps to clarify the traits of theirs that are central. The epithets may not actually appear in the piece, but they become your private nicknames for them.

Today consider names. Give each of your characters three epithets. Or, explore your own name. Or, make a list of twenty to thirty names and one or two qualities that you associate with each name.

Of all eloquence a nickname is the most concise;
of all arguments the most unanswerable.
W i l l i a m H a z l i t t

RESTRICT AND RELEASE

A PARADOX OF LANGUAGE is that we use it to withhold information as well as communicate it. You explain the valuable experiences and important responsibilities of your dead-end job during an interview for a new one. Your mother calls and wants to know all about your ski weekend; you omit your sprained ankle. You choose your words carefully in order to relate a particular perspective on a situation. You are selective about what you say. In some instances you practice the same withholding techniques with yourself: convincing yourself, for example, that a failed romance can be rekindled.

In the written world you don't cajole a reader into seeing an event one way, but you do select and present what encourages the reader toward a specific view. One method is to restrict information temporarily.

TODAY begin a piece in which the narrator isn't entirely forthcoming. The narrator may be withholding information from another character or himself. Either way, make it clear to the reader what is not being communicated in the scene. Or, write about the ways you withhold information from a person in your life.

Words are, of course, the most powerful
drug used by mankind.
RUDYARD KIPLING

A   BIG   JOB,
A   FEW   WORDS

ATITLE HAS A BIG JOB. It is the first thing we read. It gets our attention and highlights the tenor of the piece. It's shorthand for the tone, perspective, and content. One writer I know considers the title to be a self-contained poem, as is "The Eye Like a Strange Balloon Mounts Towards Infinity," the title of a drawing by Odilon Redon.

Whether it occurs to you first, last, or somewhere in the middle of a piece, the title comes when you become clear about the intention of the writing. Usually when folks give me an untitled piece they aren't completely sure what it's about. If you don't give the title its due consideration, it's like calling a person the senior vice president and sending him out to get coffee.

To demonstrate the significance of titles, I have folks swap titles of short pieces they have written and then read the works aloud with the new, borrowed titles. The results are often funny and change the way the tone and slant of the writing are understood.

TODAY play with titles. Exchange the titles of two pieces and see if the borrowed titles offer an interesting new slant on the pieces; use a line or phrase from a piece as a title and notice how it affects the tone; write down the first ten to fifteen titles on the bookshelves where your literary works live and incorporate these self-contained poems into one longer poem.

> Words are small shapes in the gorgeous
> chaos of the world. But they are shapes,
> they bring the world into focus, they
> corral ideas, they hone thoughts, they
> paint watercolors of perception.
> DIANE ACKERMAN

S U R P R I S E !

IN A WAY, all creative writing is about the unexpected. Speakers in poems and essays and characters in narratives are coping with a series of surprises as they move through life, just as we are. The unexpected happens or the expected happens but the reaction is a surprise. We surprise ourselves and we surprise one another. The only thing that isn't surprising is that we continue to be surprised.

*T*ODAY *write a scenario in which a character from one of your pieces receives unexpected news. Where does it come from, how does s/he take it, who will s/he tell or conceal it from? Or, write about a time when you surprised someone with your actions or were surprised by someone else's. Or, make a list of what doesn't surprise you anymore and what still surprises you; see if anything on the list inspires a new piece.*

To be surprised, to wonder, is to begin
to understand.
J O S É   O R T E G A   Y   G A S S E T

A SENTENCE: THE LONG AND THE SHORT OF IT

MOST OF US favor two to three sentence structures when we write. You may write subject–verb–object and compound sentences: *The rain beat against the door, and he could sleep.* Or, sentences beginning with a gerund phrase: *Eating with gusto, he finished off a pint of chocolate ice cream.* The patterns of your sentences are a part of your style and voice, but using the same patterns out of habit can confine and weaken your writing. If you cultivate a full range of possibilities you can make choices depending on your subject, audience, and purpose. For instance, the impact of a short sentence after a very long one is arresting. Experimenting increases your skill with pacing and movement.

Most of us also lean on one or two structures to tell stories. Think of a sentence as an extremely short story: it has a beginning, middle, and end, is self-contained, and something happens. Exploring various ways to construct a sentence is an exercise ground for structuring narratives.

TODAY experiment with sentence structure by writing the longest grammatically correct sentence that you can; see if you can use the whole page or make the sentence take up fifty lines of a poem. Next, either rewrite the piece, breaking it up into shorter sentences, or write a second piece that contrasts the first in content and is written in short sentences or fragments. Notice how you kept the momentum and action of the long sentence going; see if you can apply these strategies to structuring your newest work.

I am governed by the pull of a sentence as the pull
of a fabric is governed by gravity.
MARIANNE MOORE

I N V A S I O N O F T H E
M E A N I N G S N A T C H E R S

BEWARE THE EUPHEMISMS, those phrases such as "he passed away," "they are having relations," and "she's experiencing the change of life." These vapid, indirect expressions will blow smoke over significant events and objects. Euphemisms tone down the charge, dull the sting, soften emotional impact. When the evening news reports that anti-strike forces reduced the threat of non-military territories bordering our strategic encampments, it means pilots bombed hospitals, schools, and museums.

Euphemisms distance us from experience and ourselves. They are tools for manipulating language to confuse or avoid reality rather than express it. There are always those who rely on such methods to make their way through life; one of your characters may use euphemisms as a device to withhold certain realities from himself or others.

TODAY relate a significant event such as a riot, a divorce, an impeachment using as many euphemistic phrases as you can. Or, make a list of all the euphemisms you know. Or, recount an experience in which you or someone else used a euphemism in a conversation. How did it make you feel?

Eighty percent of language lies to us.
DEENA METZGER

T R A N S I T I O N S

THE CREATIVE MIND doesn't require logical transitions from one thought to another. It skips, jumps, doubles back, circles, and dives from one idea to the next. Translating the movements of imagination is one of your jobs as you journey into the second, third, and subsequent drafts of a piece.

A film director carries you from one scene to another through techniques—fadeouts, cuts, pans, and musical interludes. As a writer, you use repetition, return, association, and elaboration.

Using the word *repetition* in this sentence repeats a word from the sentence before it. Return is when the action takes place in a setting that appeared earlier in the piece. If your character is driving down the highway, notices an ear of corn falling from the delivery truck ahead, and he flashes back to a family barbeque, you are using association as a transition. To use elaboration, introduce an idea, such as loss, and develop or amplify it in the next section. We tend to favor one or more of these methods. Reread this page and notice which method I used most.

TODAY consider how you make transitions from line to line, between paragraphs or stanzas, or between sections or chapters of your work. Notice the strategy that comes up most often. Write a short piece or rewrite an existing one using a less favored transition technique. Or, write about how you or your character transition from social time to solitude.

Learning is movement from moment
to moment.
JIDDU KRISHNAMURTI

T H E   E N D

THE LAST DAY at the beach. The final week at the old house. The last time driving the yellow Mustang. When you know you are doing something for the last time you are present in a particular way. It has to do with our awareness of finality and ending.

This is also true when you come to the end of a piece. The last page, paragraph, or line is where you leave your reader. It is where you know, as a writer, that you will put the piece down and enter the realm between endings and beginnings.

Endings are charged. When you read a novel or a collection of stories or poems, does your heart race as you near the last page? Have you ever been known to stop reading and put off the final pages as long as possible because you don't want to be jettisoned from that universe or the company of the narrative voice? It helps to pay silent homage, whisper thanks, and take a deep breath to mark this ending.

Endings are the hardest parts to write. This is because they are false. Nothing truly ends; it transforms. Still, the novel must have a last page, the poem a final line. So it is helpful when writing ends to remember that you are really constructing a passageway, a birth canal, a place where the writer lets go and the work becomes part of the reader's consciousness, understanding, and imagination.

TODAY describe in detail an ending you remember. Now experiment with rewriting it so that there is a sense—character, setting, image, or dialogue—of the scene continuing beyond the words. Or, if finishing a piece is a hellish experience for you, describe the experience and your state of mind.

By the time you read these words, the *I* that wrote them will have forgotten what *it* was, though the *it* lingers on, haunting the paper, unheard until you happen across it and your energy field activates it.

MARGARET ATWOOD

Major
Accomplishments

COMPLETING ANY PIECE of creative writing is a major accomplishment whether or not it is your best piece or gets published. First of all, you can learn something from every piece you bring to a close. Second, a finished piece is proof that you are committed to writing, that you will not give up, and that you are capable of realizing writing goals.

Each piece you complete is an act of faith in the process and value of creativity, a great big Molly Bloom yes to your curious, creative, courageous side, your belief that your own thoughts, emotions, and perspectives are worth, first and foremost, your own time and second, worth that of others.

Make no mistake: Writing is an aggressive act because you aren't leaving well enough alone. Some people will love you for it and others will feel threatened by your nerve. Whenever you write you reject being a passive receiver or a victim. When you finish a piece, you're refusing to be silenced or ignored. Writing is brave.

TODAY gather all the pieces you have completed: poems, essays, stories, plays, chapters, journal entries, first drafts. If they aren't organized and indexed, order them now. If they are organized, select two or three pieces that you love and feel would be appreciated by particular people in your life. Make any small changes that occur to you and send the pieces to those people. When you're finished, get up and do a little dance to celebrate all the brave work you've done, and the work that lies ahead.

> . . . always the wish that you may find patience enough in
> yourself to endure, and simplicity enough to believe; that you
> may acquire more and more confidence in that which is
> difficult, and in your solitude among others.
> RAINER MARIA RILKE

INDEX

This index is arranged by subject.

Bonni Goldberg is an award-winning poet and writer. She has taught creative writing at The Johns Hopkins University and University of Baltimore, and leads creative-writing workshops across the country. She lives in Baltimore.